Endorsem

He who writes history, makes history. Tommy Welchel, the great storyteller of the Azusa Street Revival, once again illuminates for a new generation the testimonies of Azusa Street, and then prophetically directs the significance of that revival to the end-time revival and its fulfillment in Israel. Let his torch light your candle for faith and for the end-time move of God that causes Azusa Street to pale before this end-time grand spectacle.

LOU ENGLE
The Call, The Send
Lou Engle Ministries

When Tommy Welchel walked into my life many years ago now, I recognized he was a gift from God and that he held within himself a treasure! The Lord called him to hear their stories from the lips of those who participated in the miracles of the Azusa Street outpouring as young people. And then, Tommy was instructed to relate those accounts to us. He is anointed as a teller of stories, a raconteur. When you read their stories, as related in his own inimitable way, you see them; you relive them! They put in your heart a yearning for the same manifestation of the Holy Spirit and more.

In this book, Jody Keck's knowledge of the Word of God is added to the picture. I especially like the portion she supplied of Tommy's first visit to Israel and the Shepherd's Field.

DR. BILLYE BRIM
Billye Brim Bible Institute
Billye Brim Ministries

The end-time visions this proven man of God saw in Israel, from the Great Revival, judgment on many churches, and to the actual return of Jesus, will infuse you with joy and encouragement to finish your destiny well!

SID ROTH
Host, It's Supernatural! Network
It's Supernatural! and Messianic Vision

Tommy's heart to reveal that Christ's miracles are still happening today is an inspiration. During his trip to Israel with Jody and our ministry, he spent time with our leadership and family in Bethlehem and Jerusalem. One unanimous testimony and feeling that modern-day believers in the Holy Land shared is that Tommy has the anointing of Jesus in him, and it is contagious!

PASTOR STEVEN KHOURY
Holy Land Missions, Israel
Author, *In the Backyard of Jesus*

As we read the Bible, we learn the history of what God has done. The most exciting thing we learn about is HIS story! By understanding His story, we surrender our will, embrace Him and His plans and purposes for us in our lives, and allow God to use us like He used the ones in the Bible.

Having been part of many great moves of God, I understand how vital it is to share our stories of what He has done in our lives! Brother Tommy and my very dear friend Jody have written this timely account of miracles from the past and modern-day miracles taking place around the globe. I hope by reading *The River of Zion* you will be inspired to allow yourself to be used by God and to be part of the ongoing work of the Holy Spirit.

I pray you will apply the same faith and belief the saints of the Azusa Street Revival had to live in this atmosphere of Heaven. Remember, what He did for others, He can do for you!

MEL TARI
World Mission, Founder and President
Author, *Like a Mighty Wind*

It seems whenever people in different seasons of church history have sought the Lord, He usually comes through for them in a mighty move of the Holy Spirit, where thousands of lives are transformed by God's power. Such *kairos* moments are rare, but are wonderful to the church. Such are the periods that the apostle Peter referred to as *"seasons of refreshing from the presence of the Lord"* (Acts 3:19).

The Azusa Street Revival is seen by many in Pentecostalism as the birthplace of the modern-day great move of the Spirit of God. This revival did not last as long as the earlier Great Awakening, the East Africa Revival Movement, or the Moravian Revival. However, it has had a great and lasting impact worldwide, even more than most other revivals. Today, most Pentecostal movements and denominations trace their beginnings to the Azusa Street Revival. The Pentecostal Revival is still the fastest growing Christian movement in the world.

The Azusa Street saints prayed and waited for many years for someone to whom they would entrust their stories. The Lord led them to a young man, Tommy Welchel. They all agreed that this was God's instrument to take their revival stories into the future.

God has used Brother Tommy to do exactly what those saints prayed for. He has taken their stories to the whole world. These stories are not only written in books, but also on the Internet, thus being read and listened to by millions around the globe.

The book you are holding in your hands was written by our very beloved sister, Jody Keck, and is part of the continuation of the stories of Azusa Street. Jody has recently traveled with Tommy to Israel. I have been privileged to travel with Tommy to Kenya and Tanzania and even in the United States. I have heard these stories firsthand, with the accompanying power and anointed presence. Our time with Brother Tommy in Africa affected and impacted the thousands of believers and leaders he ministered to while there. They all experienced the power of God, as well as many healings.

I endorse this book for two reasons. First, because I have known Brother Tommy Welchel as a true and anointed servant of God, and also because I know you will be encouraged and inspired as you read this book. God has touched so many lives who have read his books, and I believe that the book you are holding in your hands will bless and impact you in a big way!

BISHOP ARMSTRONG KAMAU CHEGGEH
Presiding Bishop, Fountain of Life
Churches International
Nairobi, Kenya

Having seen my precious wife pray and work on this book for over a year, and knowing her love for God, Jesus Christ, and the Holy Spirit, this book has come about through divine intervention. That, combined with her love for Brother Tommy Welchel, Israel, and revival, makes this a timely and significant work. You will be inspired and encouraged reading these stories and what God revealed in the Holy Land.

STEVE KECK
Upper Room Ministry

If you are passionate about revival and want to learn more of the great miracles that God has done, then look no further than this book! My good friend Jody Keck documents the life of Tommy Welchel, whom God has used for decades to share stories imparted to him by those who were integral in the great Azusa Street Revival! You will be amazed and inspired by the lives that have been changed, bodies healed, and the countless stories of God's fire and presence in this anointed evangelist's life.

Not only will it get you fired up, but it will encourage you to hear how the Lord used Tommy and Jody to prophesy for revival in the apple of His eye—Israel and the Jewish people. If you are a watchman on the wall, if you too have been praying for revival, then you will want to get this must-read book. A life changer, indeed!

BRIAN SANDERS
Director and Producer of The Hague or Jerusalem and
Why Stand with Israel: A Film to Change Hearts

THE
RIVER of ZION

Take Your Place in the Greater Glory Outpouring

THE
RIVER of ZION

TRUE STORIES OF REVIVAL: FROM ISRAEL TO AZUSA TO TODAY

TOMMY WELCHEL
with Jody Keck

DESTINY IMAGE® PUBLISHERS, INC.

P.O. Box 310, Shippensburg, PA 17257-0310

"Promoting Inspired Lives."

This book and all other Destiny Image and Destiny Image Fiction books are available at Christian bookstores and distributors worldwide.

For more information on foreign distributors, call 717-532-3040.

Reach us on the Internet: www.destinyimage.com.

ISBN 13 TP: 978-0-7684-6305-7

ISBN 13 eBook: 978-0-7684-6306-4

ISBN 13 HC: 978-0-7684-6308-8

ISBN 13 LP: 978-0-7684-6307-1

For Worldwide Distribution, Printed in the U.S.A.

1 2 3 4 5 6 7 8 / 26 25 24 23 22

Acknowledgments

You never know what our glorious Holy Spirit will do in a moment's time! We had only been home from Israel for a few weeks, when Tommy called me and said, "Jody, God says it's time to write another book!" I replied, "Oh, Tommy that's great!" Little did I know how my life was getting ready to change course, when he spoke next.

"Jody, God says you're supposed to write it for me!"

Such is life, when led by the Spirit. I had never written a book. Ironically, I always said I was a better communicator through speaking, not through writing. Countless times in my life, when presented with a new opportunity or challenge, I have prayed and asked for Him to stir up the gift, to pour out His grace, in order to accomplish what I needed to do. Immediately, I began pressing in, knowing I could not do it without Him. The Lord has never failed me. God always believes in us more than we believe in ourselves. He has opened a door in my heart, and has given me three more books that I am currently writing. Isn't He marvelous?

Every word in this book was written, immersed in prayer, and with no shoes on my feet. He spoke to me that I was on "holy ground." One night, I hurried to my library, which is also my home office. I had a thought that I knew the Holy Spirit had whispered. I sat at my desk and turned on my computer. Suddenly, my feet began to burn and hurt. I wondered what was happening, and bent down to see that my shoes were on. He had reminded me to take my shoes off! Immediately, the burning stopped. Our God is forever faithful!

There are many people that have been supportive along this journey, and to everyone, I am eternally grateful. My heart swells with tremendous love for all those who helped!

Tommy trusted the Holy Spirit, and I am so thankful to him for trusting me as well. To be able to spend countless hours with him, reliving the stories, and learning the history of past and present moves of God, has been life altering. To be ministering with him, and witnessing God's great outpouring is amazing. He is a true servant of God, and does not waver in his faith. I have been so inspired by his life, and what God has done through him!

From children, grandchildren, siblings, and my husband, they have all cheered me on! I can't count how many times my precious husband, Steve, was there for me. The dinners he served, the prayers he lifted, and the love and strength he gave to me, was monumental. He kept encouraging me to "just write the first sentence!" One night, while sleeping, the Holy Spirit woke me, as He often does. He dropped that first sentence into my heart. I knew it would flow from there. Steve is an amazing husband and man of God!

The intercession and support from our Upper Room family was incredible. Many times, they would lay hands on me, praying and believing for the words the Lord wanted me to write. During our travels, Tommy and I have also met so many saints of God praying for us and this book! What a blessing.

I am so thankful to all the people who endorsed this book, and to Pastor Cleddie for writing the Foreword! To have these great men and women of God take the time to offer their support and encouragement has been very humbling. All of them have lived a life of service and sacrifice to the Lord, and are mighty warriors in the faith.

My heartfelt gratitude goes out to everyone at Destiny Image. They have been a pleasure to work with and I am so thankful for all of the help they have given me. So many great literary achievements have been published by them, and I am honored to work with all of them!

I get emotional just thinking of my beautiful sister, Lee, and the sacrifice she made in helping me. One evening, as I sat at my computer, crying and seeking the Lord for guidance, she "just happened" to call me. I poured out my heart of the enormity I felt in what God had called me to do. Within days, she was on a plane, and had moved in with me to help! She literally lived with us for months, while writing this book. We had a blast! So many days, we laughed, we cried, and grew deeper in the Lord together. There were times when the anointing was so strong, the heavy Kabod glory of God so weighty, that when we went back to edit, we would just marvel at what He had done. Several times, we would read what had been written, and could not even recall writing it. I know the Holy Spirit sent her, to accomplish what He had set before me. He not only stirred up the gift within me, and poured out His grace upon me, He sent Lee!

Being immersed in God's presence and experiencing Jesus and His miracles is beyond what any of us can describe at times. I feel as if I have also lived life with the saints of Azusa Street! What He is doing now is extraordinary. Miracles are exploding and the harvest is here! My love for Israel continues to grow. I encourage you to keep your eyes on Israel, and pray for the peace of Jerusalem. My hunger and thirst for our Lord cannot be quenched.

It has been a great joy and honor to be the one chosen for this work. I have totally surrendered my life to Jesus, and have offered this book to Him. May His divine purpose be accomplished, and may He be known in all the world. I know I could never have written it, but by His Spirit. I truly give all glory to God!

Worthy is the Lamb.

Contents

Foreword

Many years ago, when I was very young in faith, while reading a Bible with margins, a word seemed to beg for my attention. I marked it and moved on in my study. But again and again, the word would draw me like a magnet. It was a word I was not familiar with, so I studied its definition. The word was *remembrancer*. Through the years, I became more aware of the value of the word, which means one who, or that which, serves to bring to or keep in mind; a memento; a memorial. In the Bible, God's covenant promises and events of the past are remembered. I have always considered men who were teachers of the faith in this category of ministry.

In a day when men have chosen to believe that science is the final authority, it is all the more necessary for us to be reminded that God had watchmen in the past, and He has watchmen today. Watchmen who are *remembrancers*.

As I read this book, it was apparent that Tommy had the privilege of listening to the stories of men and women who not only saw firsthand, but were also used during the Azusa Street outpouring at the turn of the century. As you read these stories, it is as though you are on the front row of these events, longing with bated breath for God to kiss the earth once again with signs and wonders such as these. There is power in the telling of these wonderful things that God has done!

It is like the spirit of the psalmist comes upon you and you cry out, "We've been hearing about this God all our lives. Our fathers told us stories that their fathers told them. Awake, why are you asleep? Oh Lord, arise, cast us not off forever" (see Psalm 44:1,23). The lower and the least have the privilege of unrestrained entry into God's chamber of power and miracles.

Jody has captured something important as she has gleaned from the rich experiences of Tommy. As you read this book and travel with them in the Holy Land, you too can realize the value of a *remembrancer.*

"Take no rest, and keep not silent!" For you too are to become a *remembrancer.*

Pastor Cleddie Keith
Heritage Fellowship
Florence, Kentucky

Then the angel showed me the river of the water of life, as clear as crystal, flowing from the throne of God and of the Lamb down the middle of the great street of the city. On each side of the river stood the tree of life, bearing twelve crops of fruit, yielding its fruit every month. And the leaves of the tree are for the healing of the nations. No longer will there be any curse. The throne of God and of the Lamb will be in the city, and his servants will serve him. They will see his face, and his name will be on their foreheads. There will be no more night. They will not need the light of a lamp or the light of the sun, for the Lord God will give them light. And they will reign for ever and ever.

The angel said to me, "These words are trustworthy and true. The Lord, the God of the spirits of the prophets, sent his angel to show his servants the things that must soon take place" (Revelation 22:1-6 NIV).

If we want to be thoroughly hot with zeal, we must go near to the furnace of the Savior's love.

—LADY POWERSCOURT

We cannot organize revival, but we can set our sails to catch the wind from Heaven when God chooses to blow upon His people once again.

—CAMPBELL MORGAN

Preface

For the Lord has chosen Zion, he has desired it for his dwelling, saying, "This is my resting place for ever and ever; here I will sit enthroned, for I have desired it"
(Psalm 132:13-14 NIV).

From the upper room in Jerusalem to Azusa Street and back again, God's Holy Spirit has swept throughout the world. His river flowing through us brings new life into the hearts and souls of every believer. For those ready to receive it, floods of spiritual power will pour forth. The remnant of the Lord is rising up like a river overflowing its banks and touching every corner of the earth. Jesus is looking for people who discern the times and seasons—and act accordingly. Revival is here!

The Authors

Tommy Welchel is a general in the faith. As a young man, he had the privilege of living with the Azusa Street saints, sitting at their feet day after day, listening to their incredible stories of salvation and miracles. Throughout this book, he shares with you a few of those amazing tales. Some have never been told before. If you have ever heard Tommy relay the Azusa stories, you will notice that the titles of each chapter in this book are some of his oft-repeated phrases. In certain circles, he has been called the "last living link to Azusa." Tommy rubbed shoulders with some of the greats of yesteryear, calling many of them "friends."

As an adult, Tommy received word from God to put some of the Azusa stories into books, which he did and were published in 2006 and 2013. He has traveled the world, obediently praying for the sick and downtrodden, while sharing the stories. His doctrine is "these signs shall follow." And they do. In this book, Tommy tells some of the miracles in which he has personally been involved. An expert in revival matters, he has read more than 4,000 books on the subject. Throughout his life, Tommy had a burning desire to visit Israel, land of our forefathers. He waited until God told him to go—a wait of over 70 years. While there, God blessed Tommy with many visions, which he shares with you in this narrative.

JODY KECK is the founder of Upper Room Ministry, dedicated to bringing the Gospel to a lost and dying world. Through this avenue, she has traveled the globe, ministering to and praying for thousands of people. God has used her mightily. The anointing on her life has manifested in great miracles. Her walk with Jesus has taken her many places including South America, Pakistan, the Middle East, Africa, and beyond. Jody believes that every move of God is birthed out of prayer. This prayer warrior says that we are at the beginning of an unprecedented display of the

Holy Spirit—the greatest move of God is upon us. Throughout her 30 years of ministry, Jody has always had a heart for Israel, constantly praying for peace and prosperity for that country. Her many visits to Israel have resulted in a strong relationship with the churches in Bethlehem and Jerusalem.

⊷⊶

In 2018, Azusa and Israel collided! Tommy and I met. This divine appointment led to a God-ordained visit to the Holy Land, then culminated in the writing of this book.

So come along as we take you from the birthplace of Jesus to the Mount of Olives, and more. An end-time prophecy given decades ago will be revealed! Discover the mysteries of the eternal plans and purposes of God and a revelation of Zion—the Glory of God.

Let the Holy Spirit speak to you and encourage you that there is so much more. May a fresh hunger arise and a new realm of the supernatural awaken within you, as you understand on a deeper level that nothing is impossible for our God. May His fire fall and His river wash over you as you follow along on our journey through the beloved apple of His eye—Israel.

God bless you and Shalom!

It was as though some strange, unseen cloud of the Holy Ghost conviction had settled down over L.A. Many who were privileged to attend Azusa meetings had a broken and contrite spirit with unrestrained crying. This was so unusual and unexplainable that few knew what was happening to them and why.

—A.C. VALDEZ

I never saw an altar call given in those early days. God Himself would call them. And the preacher knew when to quit. When He spoke, we all obeyed. It seemed a fearful thing to hinder or grieve the Spirit. The whole place was steeped in prayer. God was in His holy temple. It was for man to keep silent.

—FRANK BARTLEMAN

1

These Signs Shall Follow

And He said to them, "Go into all the world and preach the gospel to every creature. He who believes and is baptized will be saved; but he who does not believe will be condemned. And these signs will follow those who believe: In My name they will cast out demons; they will speak with new tongues; they will take up serpents; and if they drink anything deadly, it will by no means hurt them; they will lay hands on the sick, and they will recover" (Mark 16:15-18 NKJV).

Nothing is a coincidence. The tapestry was woven long before the threads were in place. What started as a trickle in the stream of prayers lifted on high, very soon became another mighty river of God's outpouring of His Holy Spirit on the entire world. Thus began…Azusa.

The warm breeze out of the west wafted through the streets of old Los Angeles. Sounds of the city were muted as folks settled in for their evening meal. And yet, there was an excitement in the air down on Azusa Street in the old, crumbling warehouse. Windows had been cleaned, cobwebs cleared; only a trace remained of what recently was used as a stable. Scattered straw and sawdust served as a rug for the dirt floor. Not much could be done about the fire and water damage along the walls. Pews were redwood planks set up for about 30 people.

Word had spread quickly about strange events happening in the former church. The devout, along with the curious, came to see what all the commotion was about. Miraculous events had been reported in the Los Angeles newspapers. Everyday citizens felt that if they could just make their way through the dusty streets, then God would meet them at the end. As people neared the two-story building, they could literally feel something was different. The electricity was palpable on their skin; their souls strained forward. Melodious voices filled the evening with prayer and songs of praise. Entering the edifice brought quite a surprise to the guests. The room was filled with rich, poor, young, old, black, white, men, women, believers, and unbelievers. It was obvious that more seats were needed to accommodate the numerous attendees. Hats hung from nails affixed to the low rafters.

There was no choir, no organ, no formal collection of money—only people fervently praying for revival, healing, and salvation. The meetings were controlled by God. People mourned in repentance of their sins. Crying was prevalent as one after the other came under conviction for their wrongdoings.

The benches had been set up in a square surrounding a tiny, makeshift altar in the middle of the room. On one of the seats sat a humble African-American man about 36 years old. His head was inside a wooden crate, formerly used to house shoe boxes for shipping. This man was the leader of the revival, William Seymour.

A misty cloud swirled across the floor and outside the mission. On some nights, flames of fire shot from the roof of the lowly warehouse. As the prayers began to rise, the Spirit of God flowed across the room. Men and women of all denominations fell down as if in a trance as the Holy Spirit washed through them with waves of power. Some began talking in unknown languages praising the Almighty God.

There was great anticipation and a belief that God would touch people spiritually, emotionally, mentally, and physically. So many years of hurt, pain, loneliness, rejection, and brokenness were laid at the foot of the altar. People yearned for spiritual gifts and cried out to the Lord to heal the sick. In their hearts there was only one flock and one Shepherd. Differences fell away. Night after night, God heard their pleas and answered them. Miracles exploded. The latter rain had begun; the river was rising.

> After a little time of quiet waiting, a great calm settled down upon us. Then suddenly, without premonition, the Lord Jesus Himself revealed Himself to us. He seemed to stand directly between us, so close we could have reached out our hand and touched Him. But we did not dare to move. I could not even look. In fact, I seemed all spirit. His presence seemed more real, if possible, than if I could have seen and touched Him naturally. I forgot I had eyes or ears. My spirit recognized Him. A heaven of divine love

filled and thrilled my soul. Burning fire went through me. In fact, my whole being seemed to flow down before Him, like wax before the fire. I lost all consciousness of time or space, being conscious only of His wonderful presence. I worshipped at His feet. It seemed a veritable "mount of transfiguration." I was lost in pure Spirit.

—Frank Bartleman

History

The Azusa Street Revival did not happen overnight. Many people in Los Angeles and elsewhere had been on their knees interceding for revival. These prayers were not just a quick "please send" request; they were all-day, all-night prayers for many years.

William J. Seymour was born in 1870 in Centerville, Louisiana, a son of former slaves. His father, Simon Simon (later changed to Seymour), was freed immediately upon joining the Corps d'Afrique in the Union Army in 1863. His mother, Phillis Salaba, was not freed when President Lincoln issued the Emancipation Proclamation. Slaves in the sugar parishes of southern Louisiana were an exception to his edict. Phillis was freed when the 13th Amendment to the Constitution was passed in 1865.

Because of the French influence in the area, religious life in southern Louisiana was dominated by the Roman Catholic Church. Simon and Phillis Seymour were part of that congregation. William was raised a Catholic. However, Methodists and Baptists sent teachers throughout the South to establish schools for children of former slaves. William attended one of these schools. When William was 21 years old, Simon died, leaving William in charge of the family of eight. Because they lived at the poverty level, he made his way to Indianapolis, Indiana, in search of economic opportunity.

After several years in Indianapolis and Cincinnati, he eventually landed back in the south, in Houston. William Seymour honed his spiritual beliefs under the guidance of Charles Parham, then felt called by God to California. He was asked to pastor a small mission in Los Angeles. After just two weeks, the powers-that-be locked him out of the church. Seymour had been teaching that according to Scripture, the baptism of the Holy Spirit was accompanied by speaking in tongues—languages unknown to the speaker and often to the listener. In His revelations to Seymour, God had broken the barriers of tradition. Tradition is binding and eventually accepted as truth; yet so much of it has been disproved scripturally.

Growing and Growing

Staying with a friend and not knowing where to go next, Seymour held meetings for small groups of believers. It wasn't long before they outgrew the house and moved the meetings to another one on Bonnie Brae Street. Many hours were spent fervently in prayer, asking God for His outpouring of the Holy Spirit. Seymour prayed for the restoration of the faith once delivered to the saints at Pentecost. Several in the group fell under the mighty wind of the Holy Spirit and began speaking in tongues. Praise and glory filled the air.

Within weeks, the house and yard on Bonnie Brae proved too small for the gatherings. After much searching, the group found an old warehouse, used formerly as a church and a stable, which had lost its roof to a recent fire. There were rooms upstairs that could be used as housing for Seymour and for quiet contemplation and prayer. In spite of the fire and water damage, the downstairs could be used as the meeting hall. Although the rent was only $8 per month, this proved difficult to obtain.

America in 1906 was segregated racially and economically; women had limited rights, children had few. Derivatives of Jim Crow laws dictated that African-Americans were not allowed out on the streets after sundown in this area of the country. Praying for guidance, Seymour felt led by the Holy Spirit to get on the trolley one evening after the meeting. In spite of the risk, Seymour stayed on the streetcar until God instructed him to get off in the wealthy, white neighborhood of Pasadena.

PRAYING FOR REVIVAL

For a few months, several young women had been meeting in a home in Pasadena to pray for a great awakening of God's people. They had an intense burden for revival and were determined to hear from Heaven. These ladies would not relent until that happened. These upper-class, Caucasian women had experienced the baptism of the Holy Spirit, resulting in speaking in tongues. Thus, they were no longer welcome in their home church, First Baptist. The doctrine taught by this church did not coincide with what happened to the ladies as they sought the Lord.

Just after 10:00 p.m., a knock came at the door of the Pasadena house. It was time for the supernatural appointment orchestrated by Almighty God Himself. The young ladies were in for a surprise. In a city of 238,000 residents, only 5,400 were African-American. Sister Carney recalls all of the young ladies opening the door to find a black man, blind in one eye, with a look of expectation on his face.

They asked him what he wanted, upon which Seymour said, "You're praying for revival, right?" They confirmed this with a unanimous "Yes." Seymour boldly stated, "I'm the man God has sent to preach that revival." They excitedly invited him in. He preached to them and took up an offering that was enough to rent the burned-out warehouse shell on Azusa Street. The world of Christianity was about to change forever.

At the beginning, Seymour led meetings several times per week for a handful of the faithful. Soon it became three times daily. Although he preached often, he encouraged others to participate, either in the form of sharing a biblical message or telling the congregants what God had done for them. He made it clear from the start that the Apostolic Faith Mission would be integrated: "No instrument that God can use is rejected on account of color or dress or lack of education."

It quickly became apparent that time and space were inadequate for this astounding presence of God. Soon, the building was open around the clock. Dozens, then hundreds, then thousands, flocked to this small mission to partake in this glorious outpouring of His Spirit. No one had ever seen anything like what was happening there. Within two months, it was not unusual for 1,500 people to attend a Sunday meeting. Now, almost a billion people trace their Christian roots to Azusa Street.

GOD'S PRESENCE

Revival had come in response to the saints' many hours, weeks, and years of prayer. There was an awakening of what was possible with God. His presence was the dominating feature during the meetings. For three-and-one-half years, the Shekinah

Glory cloud dwelled within the warehouse and would often fill the whole room and hover outside the mission. Shekinah is a Hebrew word denoting the dwelling place of God; it is a visible manifestation of God on earth.

Seymour made it clear that Scripture would be the norm for Pentecostal practice at Azusa. He was a meek man with fluency in God's Word, winning over many attendees with his devout manner. The gifts of the Holy Spirit, no matter how wonderful, were not exalted above Jesus. Salvation was the goal. These meetings produced a conviction for sin; thousands turned to God. Dramatic conversions happened around the clock; the latter rain was flooding Los Angeles; the holy river began flowing throughout the world.

> The meetings were controlled by the Spirit, from the throne. Those were truly wonderful days. I often said that I would rather live six months at that time than fifty years of ordinary life. But God is just the same today. Only we have changed.
>
> —Frank Bartleman

The Azusa Street Revival brought such an awareness of the one who invades supernaturally. Everything that they had seen in previous revivals was wonderful, but it was only the building blocks. The miraculous became much more pronounced at Azusa. The Holy Spirit would come, and there would be sensitivity to His presence. Revival fire went from Azusa Street all over the country and then around the world. Many other places in the world broke out in revival at the same time as Azusa. It was like a sovereign breath of God all over the earth. It was really quite extraordinary. In the last century, there has been a dramatic increase in miracles, signs and wonders. Miracles are wonderful displays of the Father's heart for people.

—A.C. VALDEZ

Revival comes when we are burdened by it, not because we are merely interested in it. A burden speaks to a desire that cannot be quenched until fulfilled. Praying without relenting and not giving up until Heaven answers is what a true burden is about. There has to be an urgency, a striving toward revival. We have to get God's attention, then He will answer our cries with a glorious outpouring. We must humble ourselves before the Lord and seek His face.

INITIAL OUTPOURING

The most magnificent events of the Azusa Street Revival were the miracles that took place. The blind, the deaf, the mute, and the handicapped were healed. Complete cures of "incurable" diseases transpired as the congregants prayed for all who asked. When Seymour came down from his room upstairs three times daily to teach and pray, some of the most spectacular miracles occurred. Such was his anointing by the Holy Spirit. The manifestation of God's power was in direct correlation with the amount of Shekinah Glory—the greatest miracles happened when the cloud was the thickest.

The initial outpouring of the Azusa Street Revival continued from 1906-1909. Many of the saints who attended the mission faithfully were young teenagers; God used them mightily. Thousands of miracles and healings took place. The spirit of Azusa

spread throughout the world, despite controversies and criti-
cisms that inevitably accompany such a movement. The river of
pilgrims flowed across the United States primarily to missions,
camp meetings, and holiness churches.

The Pentecostal fire that started in Jerusalem and touched
Azusa spread to over 50 nations within two years. As the teenagers who attended the Apostolic Faith Mission grew up, they
ventured worldwide sharing the Good News of Jesus and salvation. Some answered the call of God to remain in the Los Angeles area. These Azusa saints spent many hours in fervent prayer
for the revival to continue; God worked an untold number of
miracles through them.

As time passed and these dear people came into their retirement years, several became residents of the Pisgah Home, a
Christian community founded by Dr. Finis Yoakum. Signs
and wonders followed them. For years, journalists and pastors begged these Azusa saints to tell all of their stories to
the world. Of course, a few were shared, but not all. How can
one capture the magnificence of the unsaved suddenly shining in the glory of their salvation, the crippled running out of
their wheelchairs, the deaf hearing the beautiful sound of heavenly choirs, the blind seeing the majesty of this earth, and so
much more?

As before, the Azusa saints knew what to do—pray and wait
for God's answer. Many years passed; the decades rolled over
one after the other. In the 1960s, God's answer came. Not in the
form of a highly-educated preacher, but in the lowly persona of
a runaway teenager named Tommy.

When the day of Pentecost came, they were all together in one place. Suddenly a sound like the blowing of a violent wind came from heaven and filled the whole house where they were sitting. They saw what seemed to be tongues of fire that separated and came to rest on each of them. All of them were filled with the Holy Spirit and began to speak in other tongues as the Spirit enabled them (Acts 2:1-4 NIV).

This is the confidence we have in approaching God: that if we ask anything according to his will, he hears us (1 John 5:14 NIV).

In the same way, the Spirit helps us in our weakness. We do not know what we ought to pray for, but the Spirit himself intercedes for us through wordless groans. And he who searches our hearts knows the mind of the Spirit, because the Spirit intercedes for the God's people in accordance with the will of God (Romans 8:26-27 NIV).

Those who forever seek the will of God are overrun by those who do it.

—Reinhard Bonnke

We must be ready to allow ourselves to be interrupted by God.

—Dietrich Bonhoeffer

2

Be Patient and Be Obedient

Tommy

*For the revelation awaits an appointed time; it speaks
of the end and will not prove false. Though it linger,
wait for it; it will certainly come and will not delay*
(HABAKKUK 2:3 NIV).

The Pacific Ocean showed off her grandeur as mighty waves
swept upon the sandy shore. The receding foam left thousands of
tiny shells in its wake. The sun shone brightly without a cloud in
the sky. However, the warm, salty breeze was not welcomed by the
young boy with open cuts scattered all over his body. Dejected,
Tommy sat upon the silky sand—hungry, sore, and scared.

He had nowhere to go and knew no one in Los Angeles.
Chastising himself for fighting over a girl with his roommate,
Teddy, he realized what his behavior had cost him. Winning

the fight brought him no consolation, and Teddy's grandmother had given him the boot for hurting him. To add insult to injury, Teddy got the girl while Tommy was now homeless with his stomach growling nonstop. He had an uncle in Bakersfield but had no idea how to get there and no money to do so. It was all he could do to sit there and not cry.

After racking his brain for ideas for over two hours, Tommy had resigned himself to continuing his life outside the law. Sleeping outside was his only option. Food was another problem altogether.

Out of the corner of his eye, Tommy saw two elderly ladies walking along the boulevard coming his way. He figured they were coming to witness to him about Jesus. They were dressed modestly with their hair arrayed in the "glory bun" style. He remembered the ladies with the same hairstyles at the tent revivals his mother took him to when he was a child. One of the women was the proprietor of the apartment house he had just been kicked out of by Teddy's grandmother. Although he had only seen her sporadically, at least it was a face he recognized.

As predicted, the two ladies came up to him and sat on either side of him. The landlady held his hand, while the woman called "Sister Goldie" talked about the Gospel. Although Tommy had survived on the streets for several years, the demeanor and kindness of these ladies reminded him of the comforting ways of his grandmothers—a welcome respite.

Soon his rumbling stomach reminded him that real life needed attended to. His con mode kicked in. Thinking the women would give him money or something to eat, he went along with what they told him, although he had given up on God when he was 14 years old.

Sister Goldie asked Tommy if he would like to repent of his sins and seek forgiveness. Tommy agreed hastily and began to pray. As the words tumbled from his mouth, an intense heat filled his body along with a true conviction that he wanted to be back in the fold of the Lord. He began to cry. At that moment, his life was changed forever.

Learning that young Tommy had nowhere to go, the landlady welcomed him to her home, allowing him to sleep on her couch after filling him with delicious food. The next day, Sister Goldie and Tommy took a long bus ride to the community of Pisgah. It would be his home for the next six years. Tommy would become the conduit for the Azusa Street saints to share their miraculous stories with the world. A new tributary for God's river of revival was forming. Many years later, this young man would one day be part of the supernatural stream of the Father's glory spreading throughout the world.

Tommy

"I was born on May 6, 1943, to Jimmy Charles Hendrix and Clarence Alexander Welchel in Grady County, Oklahoma. My mother was named Jimmy because her daddy wanted a boy. They named me Thomas Charles Welchel after both of my grandfathers. Daddy was a farmer in our town of Chickasha, raising horses, cows, pigs, and chickens. When he wasn't in jail, he was a jack-of-all-trades. And, boy, that man's cooking was out of this world. He also distilled corn liquor, which would later cause the un-raveling of our family. Mama couldn't read or write, but was a God-fearing woman who raised 11 children; I was the oldest. She received the Holy Ghost when I was in her belly; He told Mama that she was having a boy, and he would become a preacher-man. Seems He had plans for me from the very beginning, although I sure did try my best to run away from Him.

Being the oldest and destined to be a preacher-man in her eyes, Mama would drag me to all the big tent revivals. As a child, I listened to many great men of God, including William Branham, Jack Coe, A.A. Allen, and Oral Roberts. Those seeds planted so long ago took root in me and influenced me more than I ever could have imagined. In fact, I was 7 years old when I saw Branham in 1950 in Houston. I actually saw that halo thing above his head, looking like it was breathing. It scared the tullies out of me! Good thing we were sitting in the back. I remember crawling under the pew and hugging the iron legs, trying to stay away from that man. Many times I complained to Mama about her making me attend the revivals when my brothers and sisters didn't have to. She told me that because I was supposed to be a preacher-man, she wanted me under the anointing of these men of God.

When I was 8 years old, Oral Roberts prayed for me, and it was televised. Suddenly, he reached up and laid hands on my forehead. Wow! It felt like electricity coming out of his hands. It started at my forehead and went all down my entire body and out of my feet. He laid his hand on top of my head for quite a while. I didn't know what it was for, but evidently, it was for now.

I went along with the plan until I was about 14 years old. My world exploded when Daddy was sent to prison, and we lost the farm. The only good thing about Daddy going to the state prison in McAllister was that he could no longer use his razor strap on me until I bled. He was a mean man. When we had to leave the farm, the only thing I could take with me was my dog, Rusty. All these events triggered my rebellious period. I no longer wanted anything to do with the Gospel and stopped going to revivals. Life was about to get really hard.

I started stealing to eat. I was sleeping in vacant houses, haylofts, and ditches outside of bars. Sometimes I stayed at home, but mostly not. I stole stuff off clotheslines whether I needed them or not. If they fit me, I wore them; if they didn't, I threw them in the trash. I broke into houses, stealing anything valuable, what I could sell or trade. I spent time in jail paying for those crimes, but that did not deter me for long. Eventually, the law was about to catch up to me. My friend, Glen, told me they were after me big time and had a warrant for my arrest. They wanted to get me off the streets once and for all, even to the point of throwing away the key. I knew my time was up.

Because of my reputation as a good thief, others in that particular business knew me. I could be sitting there talking to you and leave with your pocket contents, with you never being the wiser. My friend, Teddy, and his grandmother were from California and had asked me to go back with them to Venice Beach to continue our thievery. Although California held no appeal to me, I decided it was my only way to stay out of prison. I left Oklahoma at 17 with the clothes on my back and a couple of boxes of ill-gotten loot. I was on the run—straight into the arms of the Almighty."

PISGAH

In 1895, Dr. Finis Yoakum opened a mission in Highland Park, a town about five miles from Los Angeles. After his miraculous healing from a devastating injury, God gave him visions telling him to open a facility for the needy. He promised to spend the rest of his life serving the social outcasts, the poor, and the sick. He was an early Pentecostal evangelist.

During the years of the Azusa Street Revival, Dr. Yoakum and his wife, Mary, hosted many of the attendees at the Pisgah Home. What started as a home that housed eight people turned into a group of dozens of cottages, able to provide for 150. If there wasn't room in the cottages, people often stayed in tents and wagons on the property. Yoakum used his barn for church and healing services. Donations came in from all around the world to support its operations. The residents ate home-cooked meals, attended Bible classes, and were given jobs around the home.

Yoakum walked the back street, among the down-and-outers, calling on them to give themselves to Christ. One by one at first, and then in droves, society's outcasts heeded and followed the fervent doctor with the white hair and trimly clipped white beard. Drunkards and cripples, paupers and habitual criminals—he befriended them all, and to them he preached the love of God.

—LOS ANGELES TIMES, 1952

Dr. Yoakum died in 1920, but the mission continued along the same path. From 1950 until 1993, Pisgah Home was run by Reverend Harold James Smith. Brother Smith published the "Herald of Hope" newsletter and "Prayer Tower" radio show from there. By the time he took over, many of the young people who had been part of the incredible Azusa Street Revival in the early 1900s had retired to Pisgah. The opportunity to minister to the broken and bask in the fellowship of other witnesses drew them to the mission. Tommy arrived at this bastion of worship and miracles in 1960. The next six years of his life would lay the groundwork that would eventually impact the world.

Tommy

"It was overwhelming when Sister Goldie and I arrived at Pisgah. I couldn't believe that I had plenty to eat, a soft bed, and so many people who cared about me. Plus, I was a born-again Christian who felt the love of God around every corner. I was hungry to learn more and do more for Him. I soon realized that so many of the residents were people who had been at the great Azusa Street Revival. Many of the preachers I listened to when I was a child talked about that miraculous awakening. Brother Smith, the overseer of Pisgah, told me more about the event and who at Pisgah had been part of it.

I wanted to know more, but I was so shy back then. One of the saints, Brother Carl Cantrell, prayed for me to receive holy boldness. God answered that prayer, then I started going to these saints and asking to hear their stories. At that time, they wouldn't tell me…there's no rushing God.

After I had been at Pisgah for about a month, Sister Laura Langtroff told me I needed the baptism of the Holy Ghost with signs to follow, which is speaking in tongues. My mother had done it all the time, so I knew what it was. I didn't know if I wanted it or not. Sister Laura asked me to read the ninth chapter of Revelation and see if you want any of this to happen to you. Well, I read it. Reading about things like giant scorpions stinging me and rocks falling on me scared me.

The only people unbothered were the ones who had the name of God written on their foreheads. I asked Sister Laura, How do I get the name of God on my forehead? She explained that I get it when I start speaking in tongues. I definitely wanted the gift of tongues. The next evening, a group of people including Brother Smith, were singing and teaching us old-time Pentecostal songs. One of the group, John Baker, asked me if I wanted to receive the baptism of the Holy Ghost. I truly did! God poured His Spirit out on me, and I began speaking in tongues."

William Branham Prophecy 1960

About a month after Tommy received the baptism of the Holy Spirit, he was at Clifton's Cafeteria in downtown Los Angeles. He and 200 others were attending a Full Gospel Businessmen's meeting on a Saturday morning. William Branham was the guest speaker. Tommy's childhood fear of Branham was long gone, so he engaged Branham in conversation. "Praise the Lord, Brother Branham," said Tommy. Branham looked at Tommy and passed on by. Taking just one step, he wheeled around, laughed and pointed his finger at Tommy and said, "You're the one." He didn't elaborate, which left Tommy wondering exactly what Branham meant. Just two days later, several of the Azusa saints came to Tommy and said they were ready to share their miraculous stories with him.

Tommy said, "The saints had told a few of their stories to some people, but they were waiting on God to lead them to the person to tell all their stories to. They told me, 'Brother Tommy, we feel led of the Lord that you're the one.' I asked Sister Carney, 'The one what?' She replied, 'The one we're to tell our stories to.' Many people had been asking these saints to tell their stories, people like Demos Shakarian, Tommy Hicks, and David du Plessis. But they wouldn't tell them. I was only 17 when I first sat and listened to these old Azusa saints. I heard their stories, over and over, every week for the next six years. Most of them lived at Pisgah, but a few lived elsewhere. I visited all of them and never grew tired of sitting at their feet eating cookies and milk and listening. These great saints shared their memories of this incredible move of God and His use of the willing and faithful young ones at Azusa Street.

"Another blessed event that happened when I was at Pisgah is that I reconciled with my dad. On top of that, he came to know and love the Lord. At that time, it seemed to be the best blessing I could ever have. If we are obedient, God will keep increasing the blessings."

Time passed quickly. Thousands still came to Pisgah to ask the Azusa saints to pray for them. Miracles happened all the time. This was the atmosphere that Tommy experienced daily. His relationship with the Lord became deeper. God gifted him with wonderful visions. He prayed fervently and walked in obedience with the Lord. When he prayed for the sick, God miraculously healed them. Shy no more, he went down to skid row and talked to people about Jesus. Brother Smith called Tommy, "the teenage fireball of Pentecost." He always watched the saints.

"Whatever they did, I did. Every time. The power of God would hit me. I wasn't mocking; I was mimicking. I wanted what they had, so I did what they did. You have to be hungry," Tommy said. "One day, I asked Brother Sines what he was praying for when they laid hands on me. He said they were imparting their anointing onto me. That was amazing to me. If you don't believe, you don't receive. Doubt, you do without. These are the stories the saints told me. They aren't my stories; I just believe them."

Tommy lived in the men's dormitory and earned his keep by setting up for events, mailing out the newsletter that had a circulation of 60,000, and any other task they asked of him. One day while hanging banners in town for an upcoming prayer meeting, he met a lovely girl with blonde hair and twinkling blue eyes that took his breath away. He and Marlene Ruth DeNebers were soon married at Pisgah. Demos and Steven Shakarian, Tommy Hicks, David du Plessis, and many other great leaders of God attended while the Azusa saints looked on with delight. Marlene looked beautiful; Tommy was thankful that God brought her into his life. Fifty-six years later, she still takes his breath away.

TOMMY HICKS PROPHECY 1962

"In 1961, I met Tommy Hicks, an Assembly of God preacher. Brother Hicks was the famous evangelist whom God called to bring revival to Argentina. Boy, did he ever! Millions were saved.

When Brother Hicks was visiting Pisgah one afternoon in 1962, he and I went walking near the Rose Bowl stadium, and he told me about a vision he had been having over and over. In his dream, there was a mountain, which was the church, that started melting down, and a river began flowing from it. Every now and then a giant would get up and walk out of it. 'Call them giants or generals. I call them giants,' said Hicks. He continued, 'Tommy, a lot of years from now, you will be one of those giants.' I was only 19 and very embarrassed. I told him that those giants would be him, Smith, Roberts, Branham, Shakarian and others. 'You stop. Take this seriously, Brother Tommy, listen to me. We won't be here, but you will be,' he said. I didn't realize what he was talking about would happen more than 40 years later. God's timing is not ours. I had to be patient for a while."

HEAVEN 1960, 1961, 1963

"I have visited Heaven three times in my life. Let me tell you about them....

In December 1960, I attended a Kathryn Kuhlman meeting in Los Angeles. Miss Kuhlman traveled around the world holding healing crusades. Thousands of people were healed in her meetings. Some friends from Pisgah and I were sitting in the balcony in a huge auditorium. I could see the Shekinah Glory cloud glowing all around her. Miss Kuhlman pointed to our section and said, 'I see the Holy Ghost and He is right there.' Suddenly, every person in our section fell in the Spirit. I was instantly in Heaven.

I landed on a patch of grass waving in the breeze. The grass was making a sound, kind of like a cat purring, and caressing me as I ran my hand across it. There were many flowers; some looked like giant tulips, and the smell was amazing. The closest scent I can think of is orange blossoms. Classical music was playing while the sun shone down on me. There were animals, but no buildings. People were walking by me. Everyone's face was shining; no one had wrinkles. Although no one looked over 30, some had gray hair. I talked with one man for quite a while. The best word to describe what I felt is peace.

In August 1961, I was visiting my mother in the small town of Wright City, Texas. She attended the United Pentecostal Church. Warren K. Poe was the preacher way back then. I didn't know exactly how to worship with them; it didn't take me long to figure it out. The power of God was very strong; I could feel it falling. The presence of God has a sound and weight to it. I had to hold on to the back of the pew in front of me to keep me steady. Brother Poe said, 'There is a young man here visiting his mother. If he will let go of the pew, we will have revival.' Who was I to stop the flow of the Spirit? I let go of the pew.

The minute I did, I was in Heaven. I landed on that same area of grass that was so alive. I played with dogs and horses and watched the crystal-clear streams. I smiled at people walking by and talked with them. Not too many people remembered what happened on earth. There was no conception of time in Heaven. The same man I had spoken with in Heaven in my earlier visit explained to me what happened to babies who had been murdered in their mothers' wombs. They grow up in Heaven. When I came back to earth, the whole church was shouting and praising God. My mama was astounded. They told me an unbelievable story of me running all around the church aisles with my younger brother Terry following me. They said I actually ran across the tops of the pews, never once losing my balance. I remembered none of that...only letting go of the pew.

In 1963, I was in the choir loft at the church in Pisgah. Lots of folks were in the meeting that day—Tommy Hicks, David du Plessis, Dennis Bennett, and the Azusa saints. Brother Smith announced that church would begin at 11 o'clock. At the designated time, we began to worship the Lord. I raised my hands in praise and was instantly in Heaven once again. Landing on the same grassy area, I played there awhile. The grass played back with me. I visited many people in Heaven. I didn't want to come back to this world. When I returned to Pisgah, I thought about four seconds had passed. Brother Smith and others told me that it was now one o'clock; the church service had ended. I thought they were kidding me. I had been frozen in a standing position for two hours surrounded by a cylinder of the Shekinah Glory. When I came to, Brother Sines and Brother Christopher were crying like babies.

That was my last vision of Heaven. I haven't seen it again, but I have felt it. I saw the Shekinah Glory at Pisgah several times. There have been a few times when I would catch a whiff of the scent of those orange blossoms. What a wonderful smell! Every day, I relive my trips to Heaven."

VISIT FROM JESUS 1963

"David du Plessis was an ambassador for Pentecostalism around the world. He visited Pisgah quite often. I really wanted a visitation from the Lord. Brother David told me to simply start whispering 'Jesus' and He would come to me. I went to my favorite hiding place, up in the attic of the church. I had hiding places all over Pisgah when I needed to be by myself. Since it was dark in the attic, I had my flashlight with me. I started whispering "Jesus." I thought I had whispered it only five or six times, but the alarm that I had set for two hours went off. I turned it off and then froze. It was like daylight in there. My flashlight was not even on. I thought, *The Light, the Light…Jesus!*

I looked over and saw beautiful, jeweled sandals and a snow-white robe with gold and tiny jewels on it. I looked up and there was Jesus. I leaped up and grabbed Him with a bear hug around the waist and put my head on His stomach. I wasn't going to let go of my Lord! His hand stroked the back of my head. He said, 'Tommy, be patient and be obedient.' He kept repeating that to me over and over.

'All of a sudden, it was daylight outside. I think He just talked me to sleep because that was the only way He was going to get away. I was not gonna let go. I wondered what that experience was all about. Later on, I would often want to tell one of the Azusa stories to somebody. For the next 40 years, though, I'd hear Jesus's words, 'Be patient and be obedient.'"

JEAN DARNELL PROPHECY 1966

Jean Darnell was an associate pastor at Angelus Temple, founded in 1923 by Aimee Semple McPherson. She was known worldwide for her prophetic prayer ministry. One day she visited the Herald of Hope office at Pisgah where Tommy worked. She told him that she had a word from the Lord for him. "The Lord is showing me that all these stories that the Azusa Street saints have been telling you, and you have been learning and memorizing, will someday be put into a book." Tommy thanked her for her kind words and then hid the words in his heart. Sister Jean called Tommy the "darling of the Azusa Street saints"; they didn't let him live it down.

⊷⊶

Tommy carried on his walk with God. For 18 years he had a prison ministry. Having been in jail a few times, he knew the sadness and emptiness the men dealt with. His profession was that of private investigator.

He visited many missions and churches through the years. He has had hundreds of miracles in his life and in his ministry. He met thousands of people on fire for God and working to build the Kingdom. One of those was Dr. Billye Brim at Prayer Mountain in the Ozarks of Branson, Missouri. She has taken God's Word across Europe, Scandinavia, and the former Soviet Union. When Tommy attended one of her meetings, he was deep in prayer. Suddenly, one of her cameramen collapsed and died. Tommy continued his fervent prayer, until he heard God tell him, "Now." He then went to the gentleman and laid hands on him, praying for God to raise the man from the dead. The man came back to life! He told Tommy that he had left his body and was moving up through the roof. He saw Tommy walk over to him, laid his hands on him, and start praying. He heard a voice say, "Go back." "That man is still well, and healthy as a young bull," said Tommy.

Tommy 2006

"I'm not one who goes and starts trying to make God's prophecies come to pass. If it's prophesied to me, I just never forget it. But, I let God take care of it. Let God show me what He wants to show me…I walk with God. If it's working, leave it alone…unless you find something in the Bible that says something different.

For years, the Holy Spirit kept telling me to be patient, believe, and be obedient. You don't know what it was like to wait 40 years to tell those miraculous stories. Every day I wanted to share them. I didn't even tell my wife Marlene. It wasn't easy. But I don't want to go anywhere or do anything unless it's God. We have to be careful to not get ahead of Him.

In 2006, God told me it was time to share those amazing stories with the world. They aren't my stories. I just tell them to people like the saints told them to me. They are their stories! In April of that year, I went to my preacher, Pastor Paul, and told him God said I could tell the stories of the Azusa Street saints. He brought it to my attention that the date was the 100th anniversary of the beginning of the Bonnie Brae and Azusa Street Revival. God worked it out just perfectly. All of those saints up in Heaven were celebrating; God was telling me to write a book. Nothing is coincidental. Oh, that excited me!

You have to be prepared, and you have to be open when the Holy Spirit tells you what to do. So, I got busy and got the stories into print. Sister Billye read my book over the radio to her huge audience; the book took off like crazy. A short time after the book was released, there was a meeting at Prayer Mountain. A lady was preaching and prophesied that the saints of God are going to pay someone a visit.

The next day I was on my way to do a book interview with Sister Billye. A vision came to me. Each of the saints from Azusa Street came by, one by one, and smiled at me. What a blessing to see those dear friends again. I asked God, Why me? Why did I get to meet all the people I met? Branham, Roberts, Shakarian, du Plessis, Pat Robertson, Lois Irwin, Doris Akers, and so many more? God said, For this time.

You have to let God do it. If He tells you to do something, do it! If I had gone to the missionary fields when I wanted to in the early 1960s, I would have messed up. This Oklahoma country boy has now been to many nations throughout the world. Obedience is your greatest success."

Tommy 2010

"In September 2010, I wasn't feeling well. After a bad weekend, I headed to see my doctor on a Monday morning. When I arrived at his office, a sign said they had moved to another location. I got in the car to go there; however, I couldn't make it. I noticed a sign that said Mercy After Hours. I pulled in and staggered into the clinic. After telling the receptionist that I needed to see a doctor or a nurse, I passed out. When I came to, an ambulance was there along with the fire department. The EMT told me that I was having three heart attacks right then and needed to get me to the hospital immediately or I would die.

I called Marlene and told her I was having a heart attack and was on my way to the hospital. She called Billye Brim and asked for prayer. Marlene said that Billye prayed for about 20 minutes along with about a dozen people at Prayer Mountain; she even announced it over the radio to ask listeners to pray for me. I then called Billye's prayer hotline and talked with a friend, Mike. I told him what was happening. If God doesn't intervene, I'm going home. So, let's see what God will do; I want His will done, I said.

I arrived at the hospital; the surgeon told me, Mr. Welchel, we don't know why we are sitting here talking to you. Technically, you should be on a slab in the morgue. You're dead. The artery going into your heart is not working, the artery coming out is not working, and your heart is not beating. We are going to operate and see what God is going to do.

I prayed to God saying that it's okay if He takes me home. He brought me up to Heaven three times; I really liked Heaven. By that time, my daughter was there with me at the hospital. I kept smiling really big at her. I stayed in a coma for two weeks. When I came out of the coma, my daughter asked me why I smiled so big; it had upset her. Do you not believe me when I tell you that I've been to Heaven before? If I don't come back, glory! I like it up there. It's up to God.

Since then, I have written a second book telling more Azusa Street stories as the Holy Spirit prompted me. There are some in this third book that have never been told anywhere. I suppose that is why God didn't let me come to Heaven for good; He still needed me to do a little more work for Him. Like take a trip to Israel and share it in this book. All my life I had dreamed of going to Israel. God told me to be patient and one day He would bring someone into my life to take me there. I prayed for so many years to visit the Holy Land.

I was privileged to sit at the feet of those dear old saints. The manifestations of God on earth are amazing, but we must always keep our eyes on Him. I was honored to meet some of the greatest men and women of God who have walked this earth. But what I get most excited about is that this omnipotent God, He's living in me! I get thrilled. Holy God chooses to dwell in me; I find that so awesome! Let me tell you about Sister Goldie and Sister Carney...."

Azusa

Sister Goldie

"I mentioned that Sister Goldie witnessed to me in Venice Beach then led me to the Lord. She took me to Pisgah to live, and from that day on, she spoiled me rotten. She bought me my first Bible, and my first suit and dress shoes. I was her "little project." At times, she even referred to me as her son, which was funny since she was a little, bitty woman and I was 6' 2" tall. Once a month, Sister Goldie would leave Venice Beach where she lived and come to Pisgah to visit the other saints and tell me stories. She even brought cookies and milk for me! In the back of the dining hall, there were couches and chairs where we would meet. After a few months, she drew an audience anxious to hear about the mighty works of God. She loved reliving those wonderful days she spent at Azusa serving the Lord.

Sister Goldie was only 18 years old when she attended Azusa Street and was used by the Holy Spirit to heal people. She was drawn to those with obvious disfigurements; this included growths on their faces. As she prayed for those unfortunate folks, the tumors or growths would literally fall off in her hand. She began carrying around towels and a dust pan. If necessary, she bandaged the area if a wound was left in place of the growth. Not all healings were instantaneous; the growth would come off, but it sometimes took a few hours or overnight for the skin to look completely normal. Most people would tolerate small growths on their face, but Sister Goldie would say, "God can clean this up. That's a mess. That's ugly, and God doesn't want you being a mess or ugly." During the two years Sister Goldie attended Azusa Street, she was instrumental in healing over 3,000 tumors and facial growths. What a faithful servant to God she was!

Sister Carney

Sister Carney was 17 years old when William Seymour came to the door of the apartment where she and her friends were praying for revival. From that day forward until they padlocked the Azusa Street Mission, she was a member of that body of saints. When I met Sister Carney, she was in her mid-70s with a slender build standing about 5' 9" tall. She had gray hair with a glory bun sitting on top of her head and always wore a pleasant smile. I had the honor of sitting at Sister Carney's feet, drinking milk and eating cookies, while she revealed her amazing stories of the miracles at Azusa Street. She told those stories in better detail than any of the other saints. The excitement in her voice had not dimmed in the 60 years since the events took place. She witnessed many miracles, but the first one that resulted from her fervent prayers is one of my favorites.

A woman had caught her husband cheating with another woman. She and the adulterous woman got into a fight. The woman bit off her ear. She entered the meeting room with a bloody bandage on the side of her head. She was in great pain, and did not have the ear with her. Sister Carney pulled the bandage off to see the terrible wound. She immediately began to pray for the distraught woman. Right before her very eyes, she witnessed a brand-new ear growing out. She exclaimed, 'Oh, my God!' Sister Carney was there at the very beginning of the revival. So many people came to God, and so many became ministers."

⊶⊰

A good story can take us places where we have never gone before. Stories, whether written or oral, can inspire us, stir our imagination, or encourage us to believe that the extraordinary and supernatural is possible. A great story can ignite the spark inside us leading to a burning desire to learn more, see more, do more. Stories are powerful! The story of life that began in the Garden of Eden is still being written today. Every day we have a new opportunity to interact with our Lord. These miraculous stories that the Azusa Street saints told to Tommy over six decades ago still encourage people to seek healing, salvation and revival!

You did not choose me, but I chose you and appointed you so that you might go and bear fruit—fruit that will last—and so that whatever you ask in my name, the Father will give you (John 15:16 NIV).

Blessed are all who fear the Lord, who walk in obedience to him (Psalm 128:1 NIV).

Observe what the Lord your God requires: Walk in obedience to him, and keep his decrees and commands, his laws and regulations, as written in the Law of Moses. Do this so that you may prosper in all you do and wherever you go (1 Kings 2:3 NIV).

Every experience God gives us, every person He puts in our lives is the perfect preparation for the future that only He can see.

—Corrie Ten Boom

God is not about using the mighty, but the willing. He is not into using amazing people, just ones who are prepared to lay down their lives to Him. God is not looking for extraordinary, exceptionally gifted people, just laid-down lovers of Jesus who will carry His glory with transparency and not take it for themselves.

—Heidi Baker

3

God's Perfect Timing

Tommy and Jody

*In their hearts humans plan their course,
but the Lord establishes their steps*
(PROVERBS 16:9 NIV).

Dawn broke through with barely a notice. The inky sky turned gray as snow clouds swept through. A fierce wind could be heard whipping among the bare trees. I had been awake since 5 a.m. studying the Bible. Deep in prayer, I heard the Holy Spirit speak to me, "Pray like they prayed at Bonnie Brae." I have always had a hunger for souls and a passion for revival. I knew about the Azusa Street Revival, but this word from God gave me an immediate desire to learn more.

Searching the internet, I found many articles about that great awakening. I came across a book written by a man who had heard, firsthand, the stories of the miracles that took place. I ordered it, knowing it would help quench my thirst for knowledge, never knowing it would lead me to an incredible friendship with a great general in the faith, and change my life forever.

I accepted Jesus as my Savior as a young woman, and have been in ministry for 30 years. Jesus has been my magnificent obsession for decades. I have ministered to women's groups and churches, traveling around the world. I also sit on numerous Christian ministry advisory boards, including Holy Land Missions in Israel. What an honor to minister with Pastor Steve Khoury, a true warrior on the front lines. I have always had a great love for Israel. I believe we are called to stand for holiness and that the supernatural lifestyle is part of the normal Christian life. God speaks to me quite often through visions and dreams, and I am privileged to be an intercessor for the Lord.

So often, what God does for us, depends on us. We are the only limit to His power within us. Nothing ordinary will satisfy us after God gives us a new life. Once we are in His will, all things are possible. When we pray, we have the assurance that our prayers will be answered. When we offer ourselves as a host for the Holy Spirit, our lives will never be the same. I can think of no thought more exciting than that the Almighty God, the Creator of the universe, dwells in my heart and will use me for His glory. Jesus ordains our destiny, but we must be willing to surrender our hearts and obey Him. We have to be "Kingdom first" believers. We must not waste time on temporary things. Each moment of our lives should be spent with an eternal perspective in mind—it will arrive much more quickly than we know.

With that in mind, my heart yearns for an awakening for God's people. I pray that His Spirit will move like fire throughout the world. I envision millions of people repenting before the Lord and getting right with God. This transformation will lead to believers stepping forward to fulfill the Great Commission. As His Church is filled with true Pentecostal power, Jesus will bring incredible miracles, signs, and wonders. Revival focuses present-minded people on the eternal reality and always begins in us, individually. This will lead to real reformation.

One night, the Lord gave me a dream and a commission. He told me to start a nonprofit ministry for His glory. He even showed me the name on the door, Upper Room Ministry. My husband, Steve, and I bought a building, renovated it, and URM was born. Our main work involves Pakistan, Africa, Indonesia, Israel, and the United States.

I love to bring great men and women of faith to Kentucky to share their knowledge of God. And, I am a firm believer in God's perfect timing. All of this led to my Bible study on that gloomy February morning in 2018.

When the Azusa Street book arrived, I devoured it. From that moment on, the fire that burned in me could not be dampened. Reading the stories stirred such hunger for more of the Lord. I needed to meet the man who told those stories—Tommy Welchel. In our lives, we have all kinds of relationships: work, friends, loved ones, and more. However, the ones who most benefit the Kingdom of God are "divine relationships." These people are sent by God to help each other on our journeys with Him. These divine relationships are few and far between, but what a gift they are!

I arranged for Tommy to come to Somerset in late September 2018, to tell the marvelous stories to us. The minute he stepped off the plane, we both knew the Lord was weaving His tapestry. I knew in my spirit that there was a supernatural purpose for this divine relationship. In one of our meetings, we had 16 different churches represented. It was an incredible time in God's presence, with the Shekinah Glory manifesting. Hearts were stirred, and Jesus healed many.

One evening during Tommy's visit, the Holy Spirit spoke to me so strongly. I knew that I was supposed to take Tommy to Israel. I was excited for this opportunity and hoped he would say yes. I asked him if he had been to the Holy Land. Although he had been invited many times through the years, he had always politely declined. God told him that he was to be patient and He would send the perfect person for him to experience Israel with. He had waited almost all his life! When I asked him, the Holy Spirit immediately spoke to him and told him that I was indeed the one he was supposed to go with. He said yes! How thrilled I was to honor this great man by taking him to Israel and spending time with him where Jesus walked.

> *Wait for the Lord; be strong and take heart and wait for the Lord* (Psalm 27:14 NIV).

Tommy explained, "Sometimes we get ahead of God's timing… that is one of our biggest problems. I don't want to push; I want His perfect timing. I have learned in my life to wait on the Lord. I looked forward to going to Kentucky to meet Jody and Steve. It's always a blessing to get to tell the stories of my dear friends' encounters with God. During my four days in Somerset, Jody and I had some great conversations and prayers. When she told me about her love for Israel, I agreed. Israel is the key in the end-times. I patiently waited for decades for God to send me to Israel."

Tommy continued, "Since I was 7 years old, I had a yearning to go see the Holy Land. God sets everything in order. I never hinted for Jody to take me to Israel. When she told me she would take me, I knew it was God. After 70 years of waiting, He said she's the one I was supposed to go with. I feel a sweet and very godly spirit around Jody. I trust her and know she's used of God. At the prompting of the Holy Spirit, I said yes to her invitation to Israel. I believe she will be blessed for blessing me. Sit back and let God choose the people, not you. If it's God, then you don't have to manipulate anything. While in Somerset, I prayed earnestly to God for the impartation of the anointing of the Azusa Street saints to be given to Jody. Even though she is seeing miracles in her ministry, I wanted my mantle to be passed on to her, so she can continue to operate like I have done...praying for healings and seeing them happen."

Tommy said, "When I returned home to Arizona, I told my wife, Marlene, about the invitation to Israel. She was happy that I was finally getting to go. I shed a few tears at the idea of the trip; I was so excited. I felt like this was just the start of a big move by the Almighty. This was the beginning of a bigger part of Tommy Hicks' and so many others' prophecies...to break loose revival in Israel."

During Tommy's visit to Kentucky, we took him fishing at our pond at Upper Room Ministry. To our surprise, Tommy caught nine fish that afternoon! That had never happened before. It was a wonderful time with friends and family members. While the gentle breeze blew through the trees, he told us several stories from the Azusa Street souls. He began with two of the most requested stories he shares around the globe, regarding William Seymour.

49

AZUSA

Brother and Sister Lankford

"I recall witnessing two of the greatest miracles where Seymour was greatly used by God," said Brother Lankford, Azusa Street congregant and resident of Pisgah Home. Seymour had approached a man with a wooden leg and asked why he had come to the mission. His leg had been crushed at his job at the railroad yards. They had amputated it mid-thigh. The man explained that he wanted prayer for his leg because it was starting to get gangrene where the wood attaches to the flesh. He said they would have to cut more leg off or he would need to be healed.

Seymour told him that he was upset because "You have the wooden leg on. It would be a challenge for God to grow a leg out when the wooden leg is attached." After removing the artificial limb, the man stood before Seymour balancing on his good leg. Seymour laid hands on the gentleman and prayed, "Let Thy name be glorified. In the name of Jesus, I command this leg to grow out. The gangrene is gone; you are healed." To everyone's amazement, they saw movement in the empty pant leg; suddenly, the leg grew out. The crowd went wild with rejoicing and praise as the man ran around the room. Brother Seymour could not even preach that night; everyone was shouting and dancing until two in the morning. About 1,000 people were saved because of this one miracle.

Sister Lankford, wife of Brother Lankford, remembered one event that happened about a year after the man's leg grew out. A man came in with one arm missing; it had been severed ten years earlier in 1897, in a work-related accident. You could see down into the hole where it was rotting and turning black; bone was visible. Seymour asked the man, "Can you work with just one arm?" The man replied that he was given minimal paying jobs and could barely make enough money to even eat. Seymour shook his head and asked the man if he was married and had children, to which the man replied yes to both questions. "This man needs to be able to make a living. This man needs to work and he needs to be able to pay his tithe. Will you tithe if I pray for you and God gives you your arm back?" Seymour asked teasingly. The man said yes. Seymour burst out laughing. "I'm just having fun." He then laid his hands on the man's shoulder and commanded the missing arm to grow out.

Witnesses could see the bone growing and the flesh turning pink. Within a few seconds, the arm grew out, even down to the fingernails. Completely. The healed man stood in utter amazement. A few weeks later, the healed gentleman came back and explained how his former job was restored to him. He brought 200 coworkers with him; not all at once, but at different times. All were saved and healed when the saints laid hands upon them."

⊷⊶

No one knows when or where God will manifest Himself in someone's life. It can be a whisper in our ear, prompting us to pray like they did in a small house in Los Angeles more than 100 years ago. The Holy Spirit always does it the best way. Our call from God is established when we are not yet born. However, we have to follow the divine timing of Heaven. Tommy traveled throughout the world ministering to thousands, but waited for most of his life to visit the land flowing with milk and honey. The Lord placed Tommy's book in my hands one cold morning for a purpose, much larger than we knew. It was time to go to the Holy Land…Israel.

But do not forget this one thing, dear friends; with the Lord a day is like a thousand years, and a thousand years are like a day (2 Peter 3:8 NIV).

There is a time for everything, and a season for every activity under the heavens (Ecclesiastes 3:1 NIV).

And the things you have heard me say in the presence of many witnesses entrust to reliable people who will also be qualified to teach others (2 Timothy 2:2 NIV).

If you're born again, you are of the commonwealth of Israel. Israel is the center of everything and about everyone.

—Jonathan Cahn

Pray for the peace of Jerusalem and thine own soul shall be refreshed.

—Charles Spurgeon

4

Keep Your Eyes on Israel

Israel

But you, Lord, sit enthroned forever; your renown endures through all generations. You will arise and have compassion on Zion, for it is time to show favor to her; the appointed time has come. For her stones are dear to your servants; her very dust moves them to pity. The nations will fear the name of the Lord, all the kings of the earth will revere your glory. For the Lord will rebuild Zion and appear in his glory (PSALM 102:12-16 NIV).

The hot wind took our breath away. The thermometer read 105 degrees when we exited the terminal in Tel Aviv. Summer in the Middle East can be fierce. The flight from the United States had been uneventful with all of us trying to rest when we could. However, the last few hours were spent in such high anticipation, sleep was elusive. Tommy had waited for 70 years to visit the Holy Land; his excitement was palpable.

Although I had visited numerous times, it never gets old. There is always so much to see, do, and learn. It is the place where the Holy Scriptures were written, where the Scriptures all come together. With us was my son-in-law, Clif Drew, president and videographer for Upper Room Ministry. It was also his first time to visit, so he was anxious to get started on our journey. Daniel Collins from Holy Land Missions was our tour guide for the week. Many hours had been spent in prayer, in preparation for this trip. We knew it was ordained by God, so we stepped forth in obedience. I explained to them that the places we would visit are often not what you envision. Expectations are of remote sites looking like they did thousands of years ago. The reality is that most places are located in bustling parts of cities.

However, if you take a few moments to be still, the Holy Spirit will reveal history coming alive. Little did we know the visions that the Holy Spirit would give us in the coming days would manifest in the form of a book to share with the world. The land God promised is the place of blessing, inheritance, and glory. When you enter the Land, you can literally feel the Spirit of God. There is absolutely no place like it in all the world. To visit the areas where our forefathers—Abraham, Isaac, and Jacob—lived is a wondrous feeling. To gaze upon the same mountains and rivers that King Solomon, Queen Esther, and the apostle Paul did is humbling. To walk the roads where Jesus our Savior, lived, died, and was resurrected is indescribable. We were ready to tread the ancient paths—the land of Israel.

HISTORY

What is so magical about a small strip of land in the Middle East? What is it that has drawn people there for centuries? Israel is valued by the world's three major religions: Judaism, Christianity, and Islam. Israel is said to be the size of a county and have the problems of a continent. Where did it all begin? And how can one condense the history of this amazing country into a few paragraphs? After all, it is the place where God rescued a ruined world. Let's take a short walk through history.

In Genesis 15:9-21, God made a covenant with Abram and his descendants. This unconditional divine promise was to fulfill the grant of the land. He also made another pledge with Abraham (whom He had renamed) to be his God and the God of his descendants, with the condition of total consecration to the Lord. Abraham lived in Mesopotamia, Egypt, and finally Canaan. Abraham became a friend of God through faith. He went to a land he had not seen and believed God's promise of a son. His son, Isaac, and grandson, Jacob, also lived in Canaan.

One night Jacob wrestled with God, at which time He renamed him Israel, which means "you have struggled with God and with men and have overcome." Israel went on to become the father of 12 sons, the 12 tribes of Israel. One of his sons, Joseph, made his way to Egypt during a severe famine and prospered there. Joseph's family, including his father, followed. Over time, the Israelites, also known as Hebrews, were bound in slavery by the Egyptians. For more than 400 years, they suffered greatly. They were rescued by God under the leadership of Moses in what is called the Exodus.

The Exodus

The Exodus is still remembered today. Passover is a Jewish tradition that has been celebrated for centuries. This festival commemorates the Hebrews' liberation from slavery from Egypt and the passing over of the forces of destruction. When God sent the last plague upon Egypt, He told the Hebrews to mark their doors with sacrificial lambs' blood so the firstborn in their families would not perish. God then sent the angel of death to kill all the firstborn sons of Egyptians.

The angel passed over the children of Israel, sparing them. The event is often commemorated for seven days in Israel, using themes of springtime, a Jewish homeland, family, history, social justice, and freedom. These topics are discussed, and sometimes symbolically represented, during the Passover seder. The seder is a meal eaten during the celebration, showcasing certain foods.

God promised His people a "land flowing with milk and honey," which was Canaan (Leviticus 20:24). However, on the long journey the people became fearful and disobeyed God. Because of their disobedience, the Israelites were made to wander in the desert for 40 years. When Joshua finally led the people across the River Jordan, they began the conquest of Canaan and the extension of their existing settlements. Israel inherited the language and the simplified writing of the Canaanites. The difference between the Hebrews and all other people was that the Hebrews believed in only one God. The fundamental statement of Jewish faith is Shema, "Hear O Israel, the Lord our God, the Lord is One."

The people tried to live in harmony and worship the Lord. Throughout Zion's history, many foreigners attempted to conquer the land. The people insisted on raising up a king for protection. Saul became the first king of Israel. Saul failed because he lacked a heart for God. David, the next king, made the kingship stronger. He had an obvious love for the Lord. His relationship with God would set the standard by which all the kings of Judah would be measured. David's greatest achievement was capturing the sacred town of Jerusalem from the Jebusites. King David made Jerusalem the capital of the land. His son, King Solomon, built the First Temple in Jerusalem.

A NATION DIVIDED

After Solomon died, the Northern tribes decided to dissolve the coalition created by his father and him. This division ended up with the Northern tribes called Israel and the Southern tribes called Judah. The Northern tribes regarded themselves as faithful followers of the original and age-old religion. They believed the Southerners had veered off course by the introduction of kingship (by Saul) and the building of a temple to house God (by Solomon).

In the 8th century BC, the Assyrians conquered Israel, but left Judah untouched for a few years. In time, they also attacked Jerusalem, but did not take the city. The Hebrews believed God protected His holy city and Temple. This was not to last. A new power arose in Mesopotamia, the Babylonians. In 598 BC, Nebuchadnezzar seized Jerusalem. Eleven years later, Jerusalem was destroyed and the Temple was burned down. Most, but not all, of the population was taken into captivity. Many may have expected the Hebrews' faith to dissipate since in the ancient world it was believed that if a people were defeated, so were its gods. The opposite happened. The people in exile, remembering the Exodus and the promise that God made, kept faith that God would someday restore them to Jerusalem.

Sixty years later, Cyrus II from Persia, after taking Babylon, sent the Jewish exiles back to Jerusalem. He allowed the local people to look after themselves according to their own beliefs and customs as long as they remained loyal to him. Little is known about life in Judaea under Persian control. During the

5th century, the Second Temple was built under the leadership of Ezra and Nehemiah. They were determined to make sure that a catastrophe like the exile would never happen again. The way they decided to do this was to insist that the people keep the laws of the covenant so God would not punish them again. It became important to define what it meant to be the covenant people of God. Nehemiah 9 tells how this led to the heightened separation of Jews from others.

Greece, Egypt, then the Seleucids took over. These conquerors from Syria became involved in battles with the Romans who were expanding in the region. Seleucid Antiochus IV established good relations with Rome. The former Jewish Temple was turned into a temple centered on Antiochus as the manifestation of Zeus, the Olympian god. Outrage in the Jewish community was profound. It was a total impossibility for the Jews who lived by Shema. One particular family refused to compromise their faith. The Maccabees (also called Hasmoneans) led a revolt against the Seleucids. The Hasmoneans took over in 166 BC and removed the "abomination of desolation" from the Temple, rededicating the Temple to God.

HANUKKAH

This rededication is commemorated by the Jews yearly in the festival of Hanukkah. This holiday celebrates the Maccabee victory over the Greek Seleucids. The dedication of the Temple was crowned by the lighting of the Temple's menorah. The menorah was a seven-branched candelabra, lit with ritually pure olive oil, used in the ancient Temple in Jerusalem. As the story is told, the Maccabees managed to find only one container of this special oil, an amount that would have lit the menorah for just one day. Miraculously, this one small jar of oil burned for eight whole days, allowing the menorah to shine until new oil could be processed.

Jews also commemorate the miracle of the oil by eating fried foods. The most traditional foods are *latkes* (fried potato pancakes) and *sufganiyot* (jelly donuts). Before the Maccabees rededicated the Temple, the Jewish people were forbidden to worship God or study the Torah. They did it anyway. To hide what they were doing if the authorities came by, they would quickly put away their scrolls and pretend to play with little tops that spun around. Today, the little tops are still played with to commemorate Hanukkah. Marking these dreidels are four Hebrew letters which stand for *nes gadol haya sham*—a great miracle happened here.

What began as a small group of resistance fighters in the desert became an empire that went even farther than the boundaries of King Solomon. There was a brief period of Jewish freedom. The days of Hasmonean rule came to an end; a new power had emerged—the Romans.

By 63 BC, Rome conquered the land. Twenty years later, the Romans made Herod king of Judaea. While Herod was ruler, a baby was born in the small village of Bethlehem. The birth of this child was foretold by prophets in the ancient world. All of Scripture points to the Messiah in some way. This baby, Jesus, was the One whom God's people longed for and prayed for. In this child, God achieved the salvation of the world. Jesus made a way for the Gentiles to be grafted into the faith of God.

JESUS THE MESSIAH

God revealed Himself in human flesh. To see Jesus was to see God; to know Jesus was to know God; to reject Jesus was to reject God. The same holds true today. Around the age of 30, Jesus began teaching and healing people in the area of Galilee. In Jesus's ministry, He brought the key of salvation to the masses; He taught forgiveness, redemption, and eternal life with God. This was profoundly different from other teachers in that day. He shared that God supports and welcomes all people who seek Him in trust and faith.

Many people accepted Jesus as who He truly was—the Son of God. Most did not. Around AD 33, Jesus was crucified in Jerusalem and laid to rest. Death could not contain the Savior of the world. After three days, Jesus arose from the dead. Hundreds of witnesses attested to that fact. Israel and the world would never be the same. How could it? After all, Heaven had come to earth.

Fifty days after Jesus arose from the dead, His apostles were in Jerusalem celebrating Shavuot. This feast was primarily a thanksgiving for the wheat harvest. Later, it was changed to celebrate the Law given by God to Moses on Mount Sinai. Since Shavuot occurs 50 days after the first day of Passover, it is also known as Pentecost. This Greek word means 50. While in Jerusalem, the Holy Spirit descended on the apostles. What a powerful moment! The Almighty was indwelling His people! The proof of this supernatural baptism was witnessed by hundreds of people. The apostles were speaking in languages they did not understand.

Onlookers were shocked and amazed that they could hear these men speaking in their languages, when only minutes before, they could not understand these men at all. The apostles now understood what Jesus had told them would happen. They were emboldened by this wonderful gift of speaking in *"other tongues"* (Acts 2:4). Countless miracles would be done through them. This gift is still available to us today! Many Christians celebrate Pentecost as the birth of the Church.

Under heavy Roman persecution, the Jewish people revolted in AD 66. Four years later, Jerusalem fell. The Temple of Herod, only a few years old, was destroyed. At that time, synagogues became very important as places of worship. By AD 135, after the second Jewish revolt, Jerusalem and the remains of the Temple were completely destroyed.

Jerusalem was rebuilt as a Roman city called Aelia Capitolina with a Gentile and Christian population. Judaea was named Syria Palestina. Jews were not allowed to enter the former city of Jerusalem. When Constantine became the Roman emperor, Christianity was endorsed as the accepted religion. Byzantine control of Palestine was secure until the Muslims conquered it in AD 628. Israel was no more. But God's promise is everlasting. It took more than 1,300 years, but the land flowing with milk and honey was once again given to the Jewish people in 1948!

OUR TRAVELS BEGIN

Our spirits soared as we started our journey. What an honor to visit this country where the presence of the Almighty is so strong. I believe the land God promised is the place of glory, favor, and blessing. Our Father promised this land to Abraham and his seed; we inherit the land through Christ. So, this beautiful place not only belongs to its inhabitants, but to all of us who are believers. The righteous and those who trust in the Lord inherit the land. Because God favored Israel above all other places in the world, He redeemed and restored it.

Attracting the favor of God unleashes His mercy and will dramatically change your life. Some of what attracts the Lord's favor are wisdom, obedience, prayer, worship, and humility. Unity in the Church is desired by the Lord; we are all brothers and sisters. We must learn the lesson of the Azusa Street Revival and seek true unity in the body. When different streams of ministry come together, a river of knowledge flows forth. Gifts of the Holy Spirit and the river of God must always flow.

Over a century ago, William Seymour wrote:

> Multitudes have come. God makes no difference in nationality. The meeting has been a melting time. The people are all melted together…made one lump, one bread, all one body in Christ Jesus. There is no Jew or Gentile, bond or free, in the Azusa Mission. No instrument that God can use is rejected on account of color or dress or lack of education. This is why God has built up the work…the sweetest thing is the loving harmony.

Tommy said, "I put my total trust in God. I've had a thirst and hunger to be in Israel since I was a little boy. This is where Jesus walked. All the people we base our faith on, they walked and talked and lived here. Nothing wrong with calling it the Holy Land. Jesus came to Israel first, to the Jew. He didn't come to us; He came to them. We are grafted in; the Bible says so. The King is inside us. We are one. He does it through the manifestation of the Holy Ghost. That's how the Father and Son are in us. When I pray, it's usually in the Holy Ghost. In tongues. It's my spirit praying; He does a better job than I do. In five minutes, I've run out of what I know. I feel much better when praying in tongues. I do a lot of intercessory prayer. I pray in the Spirit for that person. Every time it comes up, that person was in trouble."

Many times throughout our visit to Israel, Tommy's heart would swell with the memories of those dear saints from Pisgah. In the place where it all began, it was only natural that he shared old and new stories about the miracles they witnessed at Azusa Street. What a privilege to hear those amazing events retold in the Holy Land! So often, he said, "Did I ever tell you the miracle about...."

Azusa

Ralph Riggs and Mother Riggs

"As a young man, Ralph Riggs was involved in the founding of the Assemblies of God church. Brother Riggs went on to become the 8th General Superintendent of that great denomination. His mother lived at Pisgah when she was in her 90s; I met her in 1960. During the Azusa Street Revival, Alice Riggs and Ralph witnessed and participated in hundreds of miracles.

Sitting at her feet listening to her stories was such a blessing. Besides that, she made chocolate chip cookies better than anyone else. She had bright, beady eyes that twinkled when she relayed her stories about Azusa. Mother Riggs told me that she mainly watched "Ralphy"—a nickname that wasn't Ralph's favorite—run around performing miracles. He and his best friend, C.W. Ward, preferred to be at church rather than anywhere else. No wonder! Although she watched Ralph, God also used her to heal many people.

She told me of her experience with about a dozen elderly people who reminded her of her parents. They were all brought to the meeting in wheelchairs and didn't have any major deformities or diseases; they were just old and feeble. Using what she learned from Sister Carney, as an act of faith, she raised the footrests on each wheelchair before she began praying. After her prayer, every single one of those frail, old people got up, hooked arms, and danced around. Mother Riggs was so thrilled that she joined in.

During another meeting, a mother came in with her four children. She explained that all her children were mentally ill, and she wanted God to make them normal. When Mother Riggs laid hands on them and prayed, they were all instantly healed. The woman took her family to Mexico and started an orphanage. When Mother Riggs got to meet them again, they all were normal and healthy; the boy could preach up a storm. You see, God can do anything we believe Him for. But we have to believe, and say it, put it out of your mouth. You have to say it!

Mother Riggs told me that the thing she missed the most about those days was the Shekinah Glory. She was convinced it was part of Heaven. She said it was glorious to live in it, walk in it, and breathe in it. On my fourth visit with Mother Riggs, she asked me to tell her the stories that she had relayed to me. So, I did. She said I told them better than she did! She said, "That's good, because tonight I am going home." I asked her if she was going back to Mississippi. She didn't answer, just smiled. That night, she went home to Heaven. Brother Smith, the preacher at Pisgah, brought me over to her house. She looked so peaceful with a smile on her face. I asked Brother Smith why he thought she had that smile. He said, "I believe she saw the angels coming to take her to Heaven. She decided to go home."

Occasionally, Brother Riggs would stop by Pisgah to visit his mom. During several of those visits, I had the honor of spending time with him. He told me that he appreciated the fact that at Azusa he wasn't just a spectator watching God use older people to perform miracles. He was thrilled that God used him, too. He was given the liberty as a young teenager to pray for anyone he wanted. To his astonishment, they were all healed. He and his friend, C.W., each had six or more miracles every night.

Brother Riggs shared one of his most memorable miracles. One night, a big, gawky guy in his early 20s came in. He was around 6' 5" tall and weighed about 250 pounds. He reeked of alcohol and slurred his words. Ralph felt a voice inside of him saying, "Pray for him." Going over to the man, he realized that in addition to being drunk, he was also blind. When Brother Riggs saw this, his compassion surged. The man said he came because of his blindness.

Young Ralph prayed for him, and the man was instantly healed! The man was astounded; he sat there crying and sobbing for a long while. Here was a blind, homeless alcoholic who was restored through the miraculous power of God. Later in life, God led him to become an evangelist and establish many Pentecostal and Assemblies of God churches across the Midwest. Brother Riggs said he had the privilege of visiting many of these churches in his travels with the Assemblies of God. Can you imagine how that preacher must have felt seeing Brother Riggs and remembering the young boy whom God used to heal him."

❧

Throughout our trip, God blessed Tommy with numerous visions. He will share those with you along our journey. What a wonderful and exciting trip it was! Travel with us. First stop, the birthplace of our Lord and Savior—Bethlehem.

I will bless those who bless you, and whoever curses you I will curse; and all peoples on earth will be blessed through you (Genesis 12:3 NIV).

And so all Israel will be saved, as it is written: "The Deliverer will come out of Zion, and He will turn away ungodliness from Jacob" (Romans 11:26 NKJV).

Thus says the Lord: "I will return to Zion, and dwell in the midst of Jerusalem. Jerusalem shall be called the City of Truth, the Mountain of the Lord of hosts, the Holy Mountain" (Zechariah 8:3 NKJV).

I am not a woman with great faith—I am a woman with a little faith in the Great God.

—Kathryn Kuhlman

If with courage we pour ourselves out for Him and for others, for His sake, it is not possible to lose, in any final sense, anything worth keeping. We will lose ourselves and our selfishness. We will gain everything worth having.

—Elisabeth Elliot

5

What Does the Bible Say?

Bethlehem

*But you, O Bethlehem Ephrathah, who are too
little to be among the clans of Judah, from you shall
come forth for me one who is to be ruler in Israel,
whose coming forth is from of old, from ancient days*
(MICAH 5:2 ESV).

The cool breeze danced through the fields, bringing a needed respite from the warm day. The sun had set hours ago, fading into a dazzling pink horizon. Another beautiful day had come to an end. Stars twinkled in the midnight sky. Several men sat around exchanging tales to pass the time before bed. Most of the sheep were sleeping now, with a few lookouts to protect them. The men laughed at how predictable the sheep were in their schedule. The fortunate sleepers could get a solid four hours, while the guards would patiently wait their turn. For some reason, the sheep were unusually quiet.

Suddenly, without warning, a bright light appeared, startling the shepherds. The glowing Shekinah Glory radiated upon their shocked faces. The men became absolutely terrified when an angel appeared in their midst. They were speechless and trembling. The angel said, "Fear not, for behold, I bring you good tidings of great joy, which shall be to all people. For unto you is born this day in the city of David a Savior, who is Christ the Lord. And this shall be a sign unto you: Ye shall find the Babe wrapped in swaddling clothes, lying in a manger."

As if all this had not been enough, a great company of angels appeared, praising God and saying, "Glory to God in the highest, and on earth peace, goodwill toward men!" As suddenly as the angels had appeared, they vanished back into the heavens.

With tears streaming down their faces, the shepherds finally got their bearings. "Let's go and see this thing that has happened," shouted one man. "The Messiah has been born! We have waited so long!"

They were all in agreement, rounding up the sheep as quickly as possible and setting out across the fields. Filled with incredible joy, they talked about what an honor it was to be the very first people in the whole world to know of the Savior's birth. The shepherds hurried on their journey to Bethlehem.

◄✦►

In Hebrew, Bethlehem means "House of Bread." Jesus said that He is the Bread of Life. Since bread is essential for our physical life, Jesus is essential for our spiritual life. If we put our faith in Him, we will have eternal life.

Arriving in Bethlehem is quite a surreal experience. A massive wall separates the town from the outlying countryside. Bethlehem lies about six miles south of Jerusalem. It is a city of historic and cultural significance. No longer "O Little Town of Bethlehem", the bustling city has a population of 28,000-plus. Bethlehem is home to one of the largest Arab-Christian groups in the Middle East. The picturesque hilltop city overlooking the Judean Desert is administered by the Palestinian Authority. Security checks conducted by the Israeli military cover all access roads into the city.

As we entered the checkpoints, we surrendered our passports to the guards while awaiting a vehicle inspection. Cleared to carry on as tourists, we began our day in the city where King David was born. Not only was he born here, but Jesus, the King of kings, was born in this humble village. The main thoroughfare is Manger Street. We felt such awe as we passed the Church of the Nativity that marks the birthplace of Christ. The church was built in 325 by the emperor Constantine; this gorgeous building was not on our agenda for this trip. Later, I will share with you a wonderful event that took place while I was there on a previous trip I took to Israel.

Daniel stopped at First Baptist Church of Bethlehem, an evangelical Christian church pastored by Dr. Naim and Elvira Khoury, along with their son, Steven. This church is the home of Holy Land Missions, a worldwide outreach with a passion to connect the suffering Arab-Christian communities with the global Church.

Dr. Khoury graciously spent a few hours with us and was delighted to meet Tommy. In the 40 years since their founding, the church has been bombed several times. Pastor Naim has been shot four times. These brave souls are on the front lines of the struggle for Christianity. Steven Khoury shared a story with us from his childhood, which describes some of the persecution faced by Arab-Christians and the reality of life in the West Bank territories. You can read his story in his book, *In the Backyard of Jesus.*

Steven said, "One night seven men rang the doorbell and knocked repeatedly on our front gate. Israeli soldiers had been chasing them all night for throwing rocks at them. I looked up at my father, and he told me to follow him outside. My father told me to be strong, then pushed the button to open the gate. The men wearing red and black masks were bleeding and panting for breath. They wanted my father to hide and protect them from the soldiers. My father was stuck between a rock and a hard place. If he said no, he would be aiding Israeli soldiers. If he said yes, he'd be putting himself and his family in danger and possibly aiding terror. My father had a look of compassion and forgiveness on his face. The men at the door were from one of the largest Palestinian refugee camps in the West Bank. It was located across the street from Pastor Naim's house.

Most of the attacks against us and our family had originated from there. My father told them to hurry up and come in quickly. The shock showed through their eyes as we not only let them inside the safety of our compound, but took them up to the church sanctuary. They expected to be put in a dirty basement or garage. But no, my father knew that this was an opportunity to show them the love of Christ. We gave them water, bread, and other food.

Pastor Naim talked to them about love and forgiveness. He explained to them that violence was not the answer; we must show mercy to others. He told them about how Jesus died for their sins and will free them from their extremist thinking, anger, and hatred. They were shocked that we loved them so much that we would bring them into our holy place. These were the same men who persecuted the Khoury family on a daily basis. My father said that the only thing these people know are killing and hatred. They expect us to hate them, too. But if we show them hatred, we will betray Christ. Love and forgiveness is a choice that we must make to prove to them that our God is real.

After that conversation, I went to each of the men asking what I could do for them. Upon talking to one of them, I realized that it was one of the men who had once been intent on killing my father. The next Sunday seven unmasked, mysterious men came into the sanctuary, sat in the back left corner, and heard the Gospel message. After the service, all seven men shook my hand, then my father's hand, and left without a word, as if they felt the presence of God's love and compassion in the acts they'd witnessed."

"It was such a blessing to visit him," said Tommy. "All the people I met there were wonderful. It is astonishing what they have gone through and are still standing. When I first looked at Pastor Naim, there was the Shekinah Glory over him…a glow. I knew he was a special man before I was even introduced to him. I felt like I was looking at the apostle John. You can't kill him; he is still standing. It was like standing beside John; he has such an anointing. Naim has paid a price—he will be rewarded greatly.

There is a reason for the Khourys to be there and to have survived so long. God gave me a vision when we were at the church. There will be a great outpouring of the Holy Spirit there, and a huge revival will break loose."

SHEPHERDS' FIELD

The area known as Shepherds' Field consists of beautiful terraces of trees. There are numerous caves in the region. Grass is sparse, but more plentiful than in other places. Who were these shepherds from long ago? They were Levitical shepherds, tasked with guarding the flocks of lambs that were used for sacrifices to God in the Temple in Jerusalem. When it was time for one of the sheep to give birth, it was taken into one of the designated caves. Because these lambs were to be used as sacrifices, these particular caves were kept pure according to the law. Jesus was born in one of these caves since there was no room for Mary and Joseph in the local inn.

How fitting that the ultimate sacrifice for our sins was born in one of the caves of the sacrificial lambs. In the Gospels, an angel appeared to *"shepherds abiding in the field, keeping watch over their flock by night"* (Luke 2:8 KJV). This angel announced the birth of the Messiah to these shepherds. What a glorious night it was! Gazing across the beautiful countryside, we wondered which exact spot may have been where the angel appeared that evening so long ago. What awe and fear the shepherds must have felt; what a blessing to have been the ones who actually got to hear the exciting news. Tommy sat for a long time soaking it all in.

Lunch was in a quaint restaurant with amazing views of the terraced landscape. Ironically, what they served was not the delicious Middle Eastern food we loved, but pizza. Tommy insisted that the pizza was the best he had ever eaten! During this downtime, we discussed why God chose such a small village in which to come into the world. Prophets from long ago told of the coming Messiah being born in Bethlehem. Matthew 2:6 (NIV) refers back to one of the prophecies, *"But you, Bethlehem, in the land of Judah, are by no means least among the rulers of Judah; for out of you will come a ruler who will shepherd my people Israel."*

Tommy

"Perhaps God selected this place to show the world that great power comes from humble places. If we humble ourselves before the Lord and trust Him, He will be able to use us mightily. It is written in James 4:10 (NIV), *Humble yourselves before the Lord, and He will lift you up.* The Lord will make His presence and His truth known to you, if you come to Him with a humble heart and mind.

Being humble is key. Don't lift yourselves up. Pride will get ahold of you if you don't watch for it. Guard your spirit. The biggest mistake you could ever make is to start giving yourself the credit. God won't share His glory with another. You don't have to get up and announce, I'm an apostle, a prophet. If you do, you are headed for a fall. If you are a prophet or a healer or whatever, people will see it. I don't have to tell everyone who I am; God will reveal it to them. It's just that simple. Proverbs 11:2 says that with humility comes wisdom, but pride brings about disgrace. Stay small and humble. Don't think more of yourself than you ought to.

Remember, give the glory to God. The secret is the anointing; it's not me. If I start taking the credit, then God is taking me home. Billye Brim told me I was getting pretty well known and pretty big. She reminded me that if I get too big to go to the small churches, then I've gotten too full of myself. I needed to bring myself down. God guides the humble and teaches them His way. When I was in my early 20s, Brother Bill Brown, one of those dear, old Azusa Street saints, told me, 'Love yourself, but make sure you love holy God more than you love holy Tommy.'"

CHURCH OF THE NATIVITY

Although we did not visit the Church of the Nativity on this particular trip, I want to share just a bit about it from an earlier visit. This building is the oldest complete church in the Christian world. We had to stoop low to enter the site, which is said to mark the birthplace of Jesus. The Door of Humility is only 3 feet, 11 inches tall. How fitting it is to bow as we enter one of the holiest sites in Christendom. It is the oldest Christian church in daily use. The sanctity of the site is maintained by the three churches that occupy it, the Greek Orthodox Church, the Custody of the Holy Land, and the Armenian Patriarchate. Golden mosaics are featured on some of the church's interior walls; many are lost to time. Flagstones cover the floor, however, there is a trap door that opens to reveal a small part of the original mosaic flooring.

This beautiful building has 44 columns separating the aisles from each other; some of these columns are painted with images of saints. The space around the altar is decorated with large gilded icons and religious paintings. Making our way down the stairs beside the altar, we visited the cave where Jesus may have been born. The exact spot has a hole in the floor that looks down into the cave; it is marked by a 14-point silver star. We paused to pray. Feeling an overwhelming desire to sing, we began singing "Silent Night." Without prompting, several other groups of many nationalities and languages joined in. Voices echoed across the small space; differences fell away. It was a very moving and glorious moment that I will never forget.

Ready for some afternoon refreshments, we stopped at a tiny cafe known for their *kanafeh*. *Kanafeh* is an iconic Palestinian dessert made with unripened cheese, often *halloumi*, that's baked in shredded phyllo dough, then soaked in rosewater simple syrup. It's best when you eat it warm while the filling is gooey. The proprietor of the cafe was so hospitable and generous, something you will find throughout the Arab culture. Resting after a long day of touring was just what we needed. As always, I wanted to hear more about the Azusa Street miracles. Tommy was happy to tell of the amazing events that were shared with him.

Azusa

Mother Mangrum

"I want to tell you about Mother Mangrum. She often called me her "little boy." She was married when she attended services at Azusa with her husband. She was about 5'2" tall and weighed about 110 pounds. She was very prim and proper, but very courteous, too. Once a month, I would visit her home, which was one of the larger ones there. I would sit on a huge rug at her feet eating cookies and milk while listening to her amazing stories. She sat on a large, antique, wooden rocking chair that had belonged to her great-grandmother.

One evening down at Azusa Street, a lady in her mid-40s came in, walking on her hands. She would take her hands, put them down, and push herself. Her legs were twisted up underneath her. She would throw her body forward, maybe a couple of feet. Now, she could do that really fast; she could practically run that way. She came in requesting prayer. Mother Mangrum laid hands on her and prayed. She started hearing this popping noise and saw those legs straightening out.

About five minutes later, the woman was up walking and praising God! She danced for the first time in her life. She ran out of the building praising God, but quickly ran back in…afraid she would lose her healing. Mother Mangrum assured her that she would not. The woman asked about the mist hanging in the air; they told her it was the Shekinah Glory and explained what it was. The lady went on to have a great ministry serving the homeless women and prostitutes on skid row. Many women were saved and got off the streets because of her. I told Mother Mangrum that I would have loved to have seen those legs! Mother Mangrum said, "Well, you can. She lives here at Pisgah." I thought she was kidding; she assured me that she was serious.

We went to the lady's apartment, but she was modest and didn't want me to see her legs. She eventually relented and showed me her legs. Although the woman was around 98 years old at the time, her legs looked decades younger. Betty Grable, a movie star famous for her pretty legs, had nothing on this woman! When we talked, she told me that she always wondered what happened to the Shekinah Glory. That dear soul lived to be 102.

Another miracle Mother Mangrum was privileged to be a part of concerned a woman who came in badly burned. She had been in a house fire in Shasta, California. Her family heard of the great revival happening in Los Angeles. They covered her in salve, placed her in a buggy and drove over 500 miles in hopes of God healing her. She kept begging them to stop so she could die. She was in severe pain. When they arrived at Azusa, Mother Mangrum went to help them.

She lifted the blanket to check on the lady. She said it was a hideous sight…blackened skin and bone showing through in some places. The flesh was dead. She said she had no idea how the lady could still be alive. Mother Mangrum started praying for the woman. Every now and then, the woman would get quieter. They would look under the blanket and see less bone showing. Finally, exhausted, they took her to a hotel room to spend the night. They returned a little after noon the next day. No one recognized her! She had been totally healed! Her husband said she had always been a pretty woman, but was even more beautiful now. I love those kinds of stories.

Sister Lucille

I've never shared this one before, but you're going to love it! Sister Lucille McGillicuddy was a little, bitty woman who had a heart of gold. She was quite a character. She was only 18 years old at Azusa. She told me that the Shekhinah Glory mist would sometimes come up to their necks during the services.

That's when mighty miracles would take place. One evening at the mission, a young girl came in for prayer. This girl was a prostitute who was pregnant; she was about eight months along. The doctor told her that the baby was dead, and they needed to remove it. The girl did not want to remove it; she wanted the baby.

Lucille said that it might be wise to go ahead and have them remove the dead child. "You can't be a prostitute and have a baby." The girl answered that she would no longer be a prostitute. Sister Lucille laid her hands across the girl's stomach and prayed fervently. She felt something kick her hands! The baby came alive! Lucille said the mother went berserk; she screamed and danced until other people had to hold her down so she could calm down. The baby was born and grew up to become a minister in the Los Angeles area; he led many to the Lord! I met him when I lived at Pisgah. There were a few people raised from the dead at Azusa. Ephesians 3:20 tells us that God is able to do exceedingly abundantly beyond all that we ask or imagine.

Sister Lucille would tell about the miracles performed on people who had very bad teeth, and I would usually lose my appetite for cookies and milk. She said if there wasn't a tooth, she would place her finger on the person's gums and let the new tooth push her finger up. On the really decayed teeth, all the bad stuff would come out. After cleaning the person up with a handkerchief, there would be a new tooth in its place. Even crooked teeth would straighten!

Another story she told me was of a child whose permanent teeth grew in rotten and black from the start. Usually, teeth would rot because of bad diet or poor hygiene. The mother of the little girl asked Lucille if God would heal her daughter's teeth. "God will heal anything, and I love praying for teeth." Lucille asked others to bring her a handkerchief and a cup. She laid the handkerchief over the girl's mouth and prayed. A handful of blackened teeth just dropped out of the girl's mouth and into the cup! Can you imagine what that girl was thinking as this young woman is taking out her teeth?

Lucille told her, "Now, Jesus is going to give you a new set of teeth, and we're going to have fun getting them in there." She went through the child's whole mouth, pressed on her gums, and teeth grew in one at a time. The teeth grew in perfectly. The child felt no pain; she said it kind of tickled. Sister Lucille was down at Azusa Street almost every night, praying for people. She said two-to-five sets of teeth grew in every time she was there, averaging three per night.

Sister Lucille went on to become a secretary to Aimee Semple McPherson and to Jean Darnell, two women who spread the Gospel around the world. She retired at Pisgah where she prayed for and witnessed many more miracles of the Holy Spirit."

⊱✦⊰

These tales of miracles continue to bless and encourage us today. All those saints were standing in the Shekinah Glory. Can you imagine? They were breathing in the actual atmosphere of Heaven. There is no way they could have remained the same as when they entered that mission. Visiting Bethlehem left us with the same feeling of awe, wonder, and excitement. Containing the fire of God cannot be done. Everything in its wake is transformed.

Like a mighty river, the Holy Spirit flows through us, bringing life to all He touches. As we left this beautiful city, we joined together in prayer, asking God to quickly usher in the revival of His people.

Therefore the Lord Himself will give you a sign: Behold, the virgin shall conceive and bear a Son, and shall call His name Immanuel (Isaiah 7:14 NKJV).

And the Word became flesh and dwelt among us, and we have seen his glory, glory as of the only Son from the Father, full of grace and truth (John 1:14 ESV).

Has not the Scripture said that the Christ comes from the offspring of David, and comes from Bethlehem, the village where David was (John 7:42 ESV).

Until we stand in a place where we have met God, we have no authority to change a nation.
—Lou Engle

Sin is the most expensive thing in the universe. Nothing else can cost so much. Pardoned or unpardoned, its cost is infinitely great. Pardoned, the cost falls chiefly on the great atoning substitute; unpardoned, it must fall on the head of the guilty sinner.
—Charles Finney

6

Follow the Jordan River

*Then Jesus came from Galilee to
the Jordan to be baptized by John*
(MATTHEW 3:13 NIV).

The man trudged slowly down the rocky slope, headed for the river. He had been preaching for weeks on end. His garment of camel's hair would have been miserable for any weaker man, but John paid it no mind. When he thought to eat, it would often be a meal of locusts and wild honey. He was on a mission; there was so little time and so much to do. John knew that the Kingdom of Heaven was at hand and judgment was coming. He felt compelled to tell as many people as possible, as quickly as possible. He taught that One was coming who would baptize not with water, as he did, but with fire and the Holy Spirit. Some people understood; most did not.

John's burden was heavy on his mind that afternoon as he arrived at the river. With a sad heart for the sinful people, he relayed his message. Several came forward to be baptized into the Kingdom. Catching his breath for a moment, John caught a glimpse of a Man walking through the crowd. His knees buckled. This great man of God who had cried so long in the wilderness was filled with joy. Suddenly, all he had done in the past few years and all he had lived for, was coming to fruition. Looking into the Man's face, John said, *"Behold! The Lamb of God…."*

✦

God's love is like a mighty river flowing throughout the world. Everything touched by it flourishes and grows strong. When this river of grace and mercy flows through us, abundant fruit is produced. The Bible tells us that we will be known by our fruit. We have a responsibility to share that love, joy, and peace with others. As we drove beside the Jordan River, our prayers were cast upon its waters, so they would spread throughout the land.

In Hebrew, the River Jordan means "descend" or "flow down." This swiftly flowing river starts at the base of Mount Hermon and travels 223 miles, ending at the Dead Sea. It has the lowest elevation of any river in the world, almost 1,400 feet below sea level. The Jordan Valley comprises a segment of the East African Rift System. This section is a broad, arid valley between the Sea of Galilee and the Dead Sea.

Throughout history, the Jordan has been a vital feature in a land marked by religious and political conflict. Today, the river serves as both a geopolitical boundary and a source of religious captivation. The Jordan River Valley has been farmed for millennia, with agriculture focused on dates and palms.

Many miraculous events occurred near this river. It is mentioned numerous times throughout the Bible. In the Old

Testament, Genesis 32:10 tells us that Jacob crossed the Jordan with just a staff before God blessed him. This blessing was to prosper him and make his descendants like the sand in the sea that cannot be counted. During the exodus from Egypt, God swept back the water of the Jordan, thus allowing Joshua and the Israelites to cross on dry ground as they entered the Promised Land. The prophets, Elijah and Elisha, also crossed the river with dry feet. Naaman, the Syrian captain, was told by Elisha to wash in the waters of the river; he did and was healed of leprosy. Three important turning points in Israel's history happened by this river. At the crossing point near Jericho, leadership transitions took place: Moses to Joshua, Elijah to Elisha, and John to Jesus.

In the New Testament, John the Baptist baptized numerous people in the River Jordan, including Jesus. Jesus's ministry began after that event. As we visited the river near Jericho, we wondered at which particular place the Holy Spirit descended upon Jesus and pronounced Him the Son of God. Today, many Christians make the pilgrimage down to the Jordan River to be immersed. The first two miles below the Sea of Galilee have been kept pristine for baptisms and tourism.

Since biblical times, the Jordan River has been imbued with symbolic meanings. In modern times, crossing over the Jordan became a metaphor for liberation. Countless songs, hymns, and literary works have used the river for inspiration. Water represents cleansing and life. Baptism is an outward expression of the washing away of our sins.

We visited the Yardenit Baptismal Site just south of Galilee. How glorious it was to watch so many people being baptized. In an earlier visit to Israel, I chose to be baptized in the Jordan. I was given a white robe to wear over my bathing suit. Standing in the long line gave me the opportunity to remember when John baptized Jesus in this very river. I walked into the water, praising God and thanking Him for the miraculous gift of salvation. On this visit to the baptismal site, God gave Tommy a wonderful and powerful word and a vision.

Tommy

"Things are going to start happening all over Israel. Revival will break loose! All through the Bible, you've got the Jordan River. You have to remember, the Sea of Galilee and the Dead Sea are also part of the Jordan River. We must pay attention to the Jordan. Follow the river, even into other countries. What did Jesus say…fishers of men; we must do that. When I looked at the fish in the river, God gave me a vision. As those fish came up out of the river, they became people, thousands of them! God said it will be an awakening; a great revival will start on both sides of the Jordan River, the Israeli side and the Jordanian side. I began to praise God and yell to Jody, 'Follow the Jordan River!' The nets will break. Revival will go on all over the world!"

Can you imagine the words Jesus spoke to the fishermen who became His disciples? He told them that He would make them fishers of men. Jesus is living water. We need to remember the vision God gave to Tommy when we also search for people's souls to bring into the Kingdom. Without ceasing, we should continue our prayers for revival! As we sat beside the river, overcome by the beauty of what God was showing us, Tommy once again told us more incredible stories.

AZUSA

Brother Cantrell

"Being here at the river reminds me of one of the miracles that Brother Cantrell was part of. Brother Cantrell visited Pisgah often; I met with him about once a month. He witnessed thousands of miracles at Azusa Street. He later preached for decades at Foursquare Church, working with Aimee Semple McPherson. Brother Cantrell took me to the ocean one time to show me where Brother Seymour baptized people. It was at the Santa Monica pier. They would walk into the water about waist high, then Seymour would baptize them.

Here's another story I have never told before. God let me know that I can share it. Back in the day, Brother Cantrell was at Huntington Beach just enjoying sitting on a bench watching the wild waves of the Pacific Ocean. A drowning had taken place. All at once, people were hollering, "It's useless; he's dead!" The man had gone under and hit his head on a rock. When the lifeguards finally got to him, a lot of time had passed. They could not revive him; he had been dead about 16 minutes. A blanket had been placed over his body.

Brother Cantrell left his bench and went over to help. They told him, "Sir, we don't need you…even if you're a doctor." He said to leave him alone. He pulled the blanket off. He said, "You people want to see the power of my God? How great my God is? Watch this!"

Brother Cantrell laid hands on that man and commanded life to return to him. The man started coughing and gagging! He was raised from the dead! Brother Cantrell said to him,

"Well, it's almost noon. How about I buy you a hot dog and a Coca-Cola?" The man looked at him a long time, and said, no, he would buy the hot dogs and Coca-Colas. They walked off together as friends. As you can imagine, they had a pretty good-sized revival down in Huntington Beach.

Another miracle that Brother Cantrell participated in involved me. I had a smoking and drinking habit. I knew it was not doing me any good, but I couldn't stop. One day after a church meeting at Pisgah, I found Brother Cantrell and asked him to pray for my addiction. He did so, right then and there. From that moment on, I never desired another cigarette or alcoholic drink. Everything that God does is a "wow" to me!"

⊷⊶

Like the river washes away impurities, the blood of Jesus washes away sin. Sin separates us from God forever. Sin has a price, and that price is more than we could ever pay. That is why Jesus died for our sins; He paid the cost. Repentance is the key to every revival born of God. If we want revival, we need to let the Holy Spirit examine our lives. We must pray and come to true surrender before the Lord. It is His kindness that causes us to repent. Without repentance and prayer, there can be no revival.

The area of Galilee was next on our trip. We were looking forward to seeing the ancient cities of Magdala, Capernaum, and Tiberius. The beautiful Mount of Beatitudes was high on our anticipation list. Wandering through villages, eating traditional food, listening to music…there is so much history in this land, we could spend months exploring. Every place you visit in Israel brings forth feelings of reverence and awe…even the stones cry out God's holy name. Leaving each place proved difficult.

For the Lord your God dried up the waters of the Jordan before you until you had crossed over, as the Lord your God did to the Red Sea, which He dried up before us until we had crossed over (Joshua 4:23 NKJV).

And all the country of Judea and all Jerusalem were going out to him and were being baptized by him in the Jordan River, confessing their sins (Mark 1:5 ESV).

As soon as Jesus was baptized, he went up out of the water. At that moment heaven was opened, and he saw the Spirit of God descending like a dove and alighting on him. And a voice from heaven said, "This is my Son, whom I love; with him I am well pleased" (Matthew 3:16-17 NIV).

The only Christian you want to listen to is the one who gives you more of a hunger for God.

—A.W. Tozer

I asked God to give me the power He gave the Galilean fishermen—to anoint me for service. I came like a child asking for bread. I looked for it...God did not disappoint me.

—Maria Woodworth Etter

7

Think on It

*So he traveled throughout Galilee, preaching
in their synagogues and driving out demons*
(MARK 1:39 NIV).

The little boy sauntered up to the two fishermen as they rowed
to the shore. He was there for his usual take of the day. The men
had always been kind to share tiny fish with him. They knew the
scrawny things would fetch barely any money at the fish market
in Magdala. He called out to them in greeting, then stood back
when seeing the scowls upon their faces. *Hmm…must have been
a bad night for fishing,* he thought. Dejected, he wandered up the
hill a short distance away. No breakfast for him today; his mom
and little sister would also go hungry. He loathed the thought of
going back to Capernaum empty-handed.

Watching the Sea of Galilee for other generous donors, he noticed a Stranger talking with the two fishermen. Inching closer to eavesdrop, he heard the Man tell the brothers to drop their nets into the sea. Right then and there! The boy laughed, thinking that the Stranger sure didn't know much about fishing. For some reason, the fishermen did as they were told.

Within moments, the boat began to tilt. The men strained to lift the nets. To the boy's amazement, the nets were filled to the brim with all kinds of fish. Not just little ones, big ones too! Thrilled he would eat breakfast that day, he looked up at the Stranger's smiling face. From that moment on, he knew he would never go hungry again.

⊷✦⊶

CAPERNAUM

Our day started early. Breakfast was a pastry dripping in honey along with cups of strong coffee. We grabbed oranges, pomegranates, and dates to eat later as a mid-morning snack. The sun was barely over the horizon when we loaded into the van and headed north. Leaving behind the hustle and bustle of the city, we were off to visit several towns in the Galilee area.

The former village of Capernaum lies in the Galilee region in northern Israel. Today, the town of Kfar Nahum stands where Capernaum once stood. The ruins of Capernaum attract thousands of pilgrims every year from around the world.

Capernaum was one of the main trading villages in the area in biblical times. It was inhabited by about 1,500 people and was very prosperous. Caravans, traders, and travelers passed through the village on the Via Maris, the main trade route connecting Egypt and Damascus. Today in Capernaum, there remains a Via Maris road milestone. Capernaum is not mentioned in the Old Testament; however, it is a prominent village in the New Testament.

After being born in Bethlehem, Jesus grew up in Nazareth. It was in Capernaum that He spent His significant Galilean ministry years, performing many miracles. After being tempted in the wilderness, the Bible tells us that Jesus came to live in this village (see Matthew 4:13). Here, He met Matthew, John, Peter, Andrew, and James—five of His future disciples.

It was the light of Jesus that caused people to gather around Him. People could see the glory in Him; they came to the glory to be delivered and saved. All over Galilee, multitudes came to Christ to hear the Gospel and receive miracles.

A sign of God's anointing is the ability to gather people together. The sick come to be healed; the hopeless come to receive hope; the uneducated come to be taught. It is vital to develop a life of honor, praise, and worship for the glory of God. Then people will also gather around you.

After touring the ruins, we sat under a sycamore tree and read the biblical story of Zacchaeus. It was the perfect time to indulge in the delicious fruit we brought from the hotel dining room. Daniel shared so much fascinating history about the area. It was truly a place of miracles.

Tommy

"I could feel the anointing in Israel. In Capernaum, where Jesus lived, I could see the house where they tore the hole in the roof. The roofs were flat; you can see how easy it would have been. You could almost step up onto the roof. In and around Galilee, they are going to have a tremendous revival! Jesus healed everybody. We should still have healing revivals. How many millions have been saved through healing meetings?

People came to Jesus because of the miracles. If any healing gets done, God does it. I don't worry about anything. I sit back and leave it in God's hands... the healings will come. They had healings galore at Azusa and took it all around the world. Healings draw salvations. The healing revivals in America were prophesied by Smith Wigglesworth in 1948 to Lester Sumrall. He said America is fixing to have a great revival. It took off that year and lasted until the mid-1960s. At that time, they decided to stop the healing meetings and switch to teaching. That's good for Christians, but the healings were a sign for unbelievers. Israel is also looking for a sign. I believe a big healing revival will set things off here! Even Jesus said that if miracles were done in other cities like they were done in Capernaum, those cities would have long since repented."

Magdala

The bright green fields came into view as we made our way in the area of Magdala. Birds circled over the blue waters of the sea. We were excited to see the archeological site of this former city of artisans, shipbuilders, and fishermen.

Magdala was a small settlement that began during the Hellenistic period around 200 BC, and lasted about 400 years. The name Magdala, "tower of the fish," indicates its prosperity was based on the sea. In ancient times, it was the most important city on the west coast of the Sea of Galilee until Tiberius was built; it brought in high tax revenue. It was an important trade route coming from the coast and linking up with a road down to the Jordan Valley. The pickled fish of Galilee were known throughout the Greek and Roman world. Josephus, the Jewish historian, records that Magdala grew into a city of 40,000 inhabitants.

In 2009, a local organization was preparing the foundation to build a religious center in the area. Contractors discovered objects a few feet below the surface. A subsequent dig revealed a Jewish synagogue more than 2,000 years old! The Magdala Synagogue dates to about 50 years before the birth of Christ. The beautiful mosaics in the courtyard show the city's prosperity. Additional excavation revealed an entire town, including fishermen's quarters and a marketplace. The most important find so far is the Magdala Stone, a carved stone block that depicts the Second Temple. Carved upon it is one of the earliest known images of the seven-branch menorah.

Josephus wrote that during the second Jewish Revolt, Magdala was used as a base for the rebels. These freedom fighters tore down the synagogue and used its stones to fortify the village. These stones are still visible today surrounding the town. Experts believe that only 10 percent of the ancient remains are exposed; there is so much more to be discovered. Magdala is one of Israel's most important archaeological finds in the last 50 years.

All four biblical Gospels write of Mary Magdalene, a follower of Jesus. It is assumed that her name means Mary of Magdala, but there is no biblical information to show that this was her birthplace or home. She was not like the other disciples—she was not a man, not a tax collector, not a fisherman. Yet, she is mentioned 12 times in the Gospels, more than most of the apostles. Jesus exorcised seven demons from Mary Magdalene. She was present at the crucifixion and was the first to see that He was no longer in His grave, but risen. Contrary to speculation, the Bible never says or even hints that Mary was a prostitute.

Walking through this ancient city was an amazing experience. We envisioned the worshippers attending the beautiful Magdala Synagogue and praising God through the centuries. There are wonderful replicas of the Magdala Stone and numerous paintings that can be had as souvenirs. The most beautiful print in the chapel gift shop was called, "Encounter." This amazing rendition showed the woman touching the hem of Jesus's garment. Breathtaking! Our suitcases were getting fuller.

THE MOUNT OF BEATITUDES

The sweeping view as we came to the Mount of Beatitudes took our breath away. The lake sparkled in the noonday sun. Glorious music filled the air.

The Mount of Beatitudes is a hill in northern Israel in the Korazim Plateau. This serenely beautiful place is believed to be the setting for Jesus's most famous teaching, the Sermon on the Mount. Overlooking the northwestern shore of the Sea of Galilee, it offers an amazing vista of the lake and the Golan Heights cliffs on the other side. The actual location of the Sermon on the Mount is unknown, but the present location has been commemorated as such for more than 1,600 years.

On the summit, the Church of the Beatitudes blends into the slope. This majestic octagonal building has eight sides representing the eight beatitudes, which are shown in Latin in the upper windows. It was built in 1938 for a Franciscan order of nuns. The splendid mosaic floor depicts the seven virtues of faith, justice, hope, fortitude, temperance, prudence, and charity. Standing on the church porch gazing out at the sea and hills makes for a powerful setting to recall the Sermon on the Mount.

> "The serenity of this beautiful place, however, may be slightly unhelpful here, suggesting that Jesus's words were calm and soothing, when in fact they were radical, demanding, authoritative, revolutionary, and countercultural. Jesus was calling Israel to a new way of life."
>
> —PETER WALKER
> biblical scholar

Tommy said, "Looking down where Jesus fed several thousand people was amazing. You could feel the Spirit and see the Lord down there preaching. When we sat where the Sermon on the Mount was likely preached, it didn't look real. The place looked perfect, so beautiful. The two greatest sermons ever preached were the Sermon on the Mount and Martin Luther King Jr.'s speech, '*I Have a Dream.*" He said, 'One day a man will be judged not by the color of his skin, but the content of his character....' That was one of the greatest statements ever made."

TIBERIAS

Winding down through the hills, we made our way to the waterfront of Tiberias in search of a cool drink. It was a nice area to sit and watch the boats in the marina and discuss the history of this important city. After our refreshments, we loaded up and headed south to see the Roman ruins.

Tiberias was founded on the western shores of the Sea of Galilee by Herod Antipas. He was one of Herod the Great's three sons who divided up Palestine after their father's death. Herod Antipas named the city after the reigning Roman emperor, Tiberius. After the destruction of the Temple, Galilee became the main Jewish area of Palestine. Its principal city, Tiberias, grew in importance. The High Court of Israel during the period of the Second Temple, the Sanhedrin, along with the academies of Jewish scholarship, moved there.

It was built around 17 natural mineral hot springs almost 700 feet below sea level. Tiberias has welcomed tourists from every part of the ancient world for more than 2,000 years. It is one of the lowest lying cities of its size in the world. Ruins of the southern gate of the city, which was built by Agrippa II, were uncovered in 1975. Melodious bells ring from the many churches in the town. Tommy was eager to tell us more stories.

AZUSA

Brother Sines and Brother Christopher

"Listening to all the church bells in this area reminds me of the stories that Brother Sines and Brother Christopher told me. They were both part of the leadership team at Azusa. Although singing in the Spirit was already part of the worship services there, it was enhanced when Sines and Christopher joined them. With the addition of their piano and violin, the new heavenly song went from ordinary to extraordinary. Sines was about 26 years old during the Azusa Revival.

I met Brother Sines in 1960 at Pisgah. I stayed in a three-story dormitory where Sines was the dormitory director for all the single men staying at Pisgah. I had a deal with him that I would clean his apartment if he would tell me his stories. After I finished mopping the linoleum floors, we would get my favorite snack, and the amazing stories would begin.

Brother Sines had been a concert pianist, even working at one point with Tommy Dorsey. He brought his piano to the Apostolic Faith Mission. Without sheet music or a hymnal, whatever song Brother Seymour wanted him to play and sing, he would do it. "Tommy, when I was at Azusa, I'd sit and watch my fingers move, and it sounded like a thousand pianos playing," he said. It brings to mind Revelation 5:11 (NIV), *"Then I looked and heard the voice of many angels, numbering thousands upon thousands, and ten thousand times ten thousand...."* Can you imagine how glorious that must have sounded? It was like a heavenly choir singing.

One of the miracles Brother Sines told me about was performed through Seymour. At that time, flames of holy fire were shooting into and out of the old warehouse. The whole place was full of the Shekinah Glory. This particular miracle involved a man who had smoked cigars for most of his life. He always had one stuck in the corner of his mouth. Where the cigar rested in his mouth, cancer grew. The cancer had eaten a hole in the man's cheek. In his mouth, what wasn't eaten away was black and rotten. Several teeth were missing.

He told Brother Seymour and Brother Sines that the doctor had given him no more than a year to live. Seymour told him that the doctor was right, but God could change it. He laid hands on the man and prayed; when he took his hands away, the black tissue had disappeared! They stood there and actually watched missing gums, teeth, and flesh fill in until he was made whole. We serve a mighty God!

Now, about six months after Sines had been at Azusa Street, Brother Christopher joined the congregation. He owned a Stradivarius violin and would accompany Brother Sines when he played his piano. In the years following Azusa, Sines and Christopher played many concerts together.

Brother Christopher also lived at Pisgah when he grew old. He lived in the dorm at the same time I lived there. He was one of the most polite and trusting men I have ever known. He was of Italian ancestry and still had coal-black hair in his 70s. He told me that when he played at the Azusa mission, he played in the Spirit: "I played at a level I never achieved even in my greatest concert," he said. He once tried to bottle the Shekinah Glory; to his dismay, the bottle was empty the next morning. One of the miracles he was involved with concerned a blind man brought into the meeting by the man's wife. In his left hand, he held a white cane with a red tip; with his right hand, he held onto his wife. The woman walked straight up to Brother Christopher saying, "My husband is blind. Heal him." Christopher quietly explained that he couldn't heal him, but he could pray for him, and Jesus would heal him. She insisted that he do so. Humbly and obediently, Brother Christopher prayed for the man. Instantly, he was healed!

Brother Fox

All this talk about music makes me think of all the people who have never heard singing or even the spoken word. Which leads me to Brother Fox. When Fox was in his late teens, he went to Azusa Street to prepare to go to the mission field. By the age of 20, he was performing miracles and bringing the word of God to India. I met him in 1963 when he retired to Pisgah; he was very happy to renew his friendships with many Azusa saints. He was about five feet, nine inches tall and kept his silver hair rather long and combed straight back. His hair was so shiny it would glow when he was around a light.

Occasionally, I would ride the trolley with him when he would go witness to those people riding the cable cars. In between his witnessing, he would tell me stories about India. What a mighty ministry he had! The Azusa Street miracles were told to me at his apartment while I sat at his feet listening intently.

Brother Fox said he was awestruck by the move of God! He said the manifestation of God's power varied according to the degree of the Shekinah Glory present—the thicker the cloud, the greater the miracles! Fox had tremendous love and respect for Brother Seymour, saying he was a very deep man of God.

Brother Fox loved to pray for the deaf and the mute. One evening, a sign-language teacher at a school for the deaf brought in about 35 of his students. "If you want to teach them to sign, then why did you bring them to a place where they would get healed?" Fox asked the teacher. Looking surprised, the teacher said that Fox was talking like they would all get healed. Fox, emboldened by the Holy Spirit, replied that they would! Brother Fox asked them to form a circle and join hands. Without hesitation, Fox whispered in the first man's ear and told the bad spirit to come out.

Immediately, the miracle happened! When the man could suddenly hear, he got very excited. When the others saw his excitement and amazement, they started getting healed one by one like a line of dominoes. All Fox had to do was whisper in the first man's ear, then God took it from there. In just a few minutes, every single one of them was healed! Brother Fox had a strong belief in the power of Jesus."

⊷✦⊶

Traveling throughout the Galilee region showcased the past and present in such a visual form. It was like this throughout all of Israel. We viewed the ruins of a synagogue and ancient relics. Nearby, young boys, dressed in their team colors, kicked around a soccer ball. We shopped in an old bazaar that had been around for centuries and visited an ancient seaport, but also enjoyed a snow cone from an amusement park. Churches were honed from stones millennia ago, yet modern hymns played on their loud-speakers. Yesterday and today greeted us around every corner. We wondered what tomorrow would hold for the region of Galilee.

Jesus went throughout Galilee, teaching in their synagogues, proclaiming the good news of the kingdom, and healing every disease and sickness among the people (Matthew 4:23 NIV).

Then some boats from Tiberias landed near the place where the people had eaten the bread after the Lord had given thanks (John 6:23 NIV).

Blessed are the poor in spirit, for theirs is the kingdom of heaven. Blessed are those who mourn, for they will be comforted. Blessed are the meek, for they will inherit the earth. Blessed are those who hunger and thirst for righteousness, for they will be filled. Blessed are the merciful, for they will be shown mercy. Blessed are the pure in heart, for they will see God. Blessed are the peacemakers, for they will be called children of God. Blessed are those who are persecuted because of righteousness, for theirs is the kingdom of heaven. Blessed are you when people insult you, persecute you and falsely say all kinds of evil against you because of me. Rejoice and be glad, because great is your reward in heaven, for in the same way they persecuted the prophets who were before you (Matthew 5:3-12 NIV).

You can never pray the prayer of faith if you look at the person who is needing it. There is only one place to look and that is to Jesus.

—Smith Wigglesworth

No one has the right to hear the Gospel twice, while there remains someone who has not heard it once.

—Oswald J. Smith

8

Because God Said

Sea of Galilee and Dead Sea

Shortly before dawn, Jesus went out to them, walking on the lake. When the disciples saw him walking on the lake, they were terrified. "It's a ghost," they said, and cried out in fear. But Jesus immediately said to them: "Take courage! It is I. Don't be afraid"
(MATTHEW 14:25-27 NIV).

The fierce wind coming off the cliffs churned the water, creating large waves. The boat creaked as the water crashed against the hull. The men barely managed to keep the boat on course. They were tired and weary; it had been a long night. The disciples were more than three miles from land and still had quite a distance to go. Earlier, they had left Jesus on the shore with the understanding He would meet them later. The group was headed north to Capernaum. Shortly before dawn, the men looked up in disbelief. Jesus was walking on the water toward them! Terrified, they thought He was a ghost. They had never witnessed anything so incredible! When Jesus came aboard the boat, they looked at Him with awe and reverence. Worshipping Him, they said, "Truly you are the Son of God!"

⊷✦⊷

THE SEA OF GALILEE

The heavy smell of fish reached our nostrils long before we walked down the dock to catch the boat. Along the bank, we could see small fish gliding across the pebbles through the clear water. No doubt we were at the Sea of Galilee. The wind gusting down the hills of the Golan Heights was accompanied by a sizzling sun. The waves were surprisingly choppy, making it a little difficult to board the vessel. What a glorious day we had planned. On our agenda was a tour of this freshwater lake that played host to the ministry of Jesus about 2,000 years ago. For lunch, we were scheduled for a meal at a small hole-in-the-wall restaurant known for their red-belly tilapia. The Dead Sea would round out a very busy day.

The Sea of Galilee, also called Lake Tiberius or Lake Gennesaret, has always played a significant role in this area. In AD 135, after a Jewish revolt, the Romans banned all Jews from Jerusalem. At that time, the center of Jewish culture shifted to the region of Galilee. Many people lived in this area of rich cultural diversity. At the time, this area was the most densely populated in all of Israel. Ancient Palestinian (Canaanite) structures have been uncovered that date to 1000 and 2000 BC. The lake is fed by the Jordan River in the north and empties into the Jordan River in the south. The river continues from there, finally ending in the Dead Sea. Along the shore, bananas, dates, citrus fruits, and olives grow in the fertile countryside.

The Sea of Galilee area is where most of Jesus's public life was spent; much of His ministry happened in the environs of this sea. In the Bible, we read of the amazing miracles that Jesus performed—feeding thousands with five loaves of bread and two fish, walking on water, and calming a storm.

Tommy said, "Jesus lived and ministered where there was life, the Sea of Galilee and the Jordan River…not the Dead Sea. The Sea of Galilee is teeming with life, whereas the Dead Sea is not. There are always people who will obey God. There is going to be a tremendous revival around Galilee!"

Many tours operate on the Sea of Galilee. One option was a large boat that could hold dozens of passengers. Another choice was a replica of an ancient fisherman's vessel. This boat is based on a 1986 archeological discovery found in the mud where it had been resting for 2,000 years. A drought had caused the lake to recede, thereby revealing this amazing artifact. It was 27 feet long and could hold 15 fishermen. Carbon dating showed it to be from the first century AD. This relic is on display in a museum on the shore of the Galilee and is known as the Jesus Boat.

We opted to take one of the replicas that was equipped with a motor. As we approached the center of the lake, the captain cut the engine. Drifting along listening to the waves lap against the wooden sides gave us an overwhelming, peaceful feeling. We sang several worship songs glorifying God. Gazing across this ancient sea, we absolutely felt the presence of the Lord. To know that this was the water that Jesus walked upon filled us with awe.

Starting the engine again, we headed to another spot in the lake. As our boat glided across the water, cool spray splashed onto our faces. Tommy said he could envision Jesus walking across the water as He came to meet His disciples in their boat: "How scared they must have been! But, think about how their faith increased." Faith is more than belief, more than trust, more than confidence. Even today, events transpire that increase our faith. When we pray for God to heal someone and He does so, our faith soars. Especially if it happens in front of our very eyes, then and there. When we are burdened with the cares of this world, and He comes to our rescue, our faith rises. However, it doesn't take seeing miracles to increase our faith, although that is always amazing to witness. The simple act of reading your Bible will increase your faith.

> *Therefore I tell you, whatever you ask for in prayer, believe that you have received it, and it will be yours* (Mark 11:24 NIV).

Our boat captain slowed to a stop again and gave a demonstration. He took nets that were made in the old-fashioned way, and cast them into the sea to show us how fishing was done in biblical times. The nets from long ago were made of linen; these were less visible to fish, so fishing could also be done at nighttime. Today, the sea still teams with fish, although tourists are not allowed to catch them. However, as a special treat, our captain allowed Tommy to fish in the sea with a pole, as long as he threw back his catch.

Of the 27 species of fish in the Sea of Galilee, the best-known is tilapia, nicknamed St. Peter's Fish. The name refers to the biblical passage in which temple tax collectors ask Peter if Jesus pays the temple tax. Jesus instructs Peter to go fishing. The fish Peter caught had the coin in it for the taxes.

But so that we may not cause offense, go to the lake and throw out your line. Take the first fish you catch; open its mouth and you will find a four-drachma coin. Take it and give it to them for my tax and yours (Matthew 17:27 NIV).

When Jesus was selecting His disciples, He came upon two brothers fishing in the Sea of Galilee. Jesus told Simon and Andrew to follow Him, and He would make them fishers of men. *"Come, follow me,' Jesus said, 'and I will send you out to fish for people"* (Matthew 4:19; Mark 1:17 NIV). We need to follow that same mandate today. We need to bring as many people as possible into the Kingdom. Time is of the essence. As you will recall, God gave Tommy a vision at the Jordan River that a great revival will start there. We must remember this vision as we fish for souls to bring to the Lord!

As Tommy looked to the hills, he could see where the demon-infested swine ran off the cliff, plunging into the sea and destroying the demons, "We all have authority over demons. They have to do what we tell them to do. Demons are not that powerful, unless you let them be. I don't bat an eye over it," he told us.

Our boat ride went far too quickly, but we sure were hungry. Bidding a temporary farewell to the Sea of Galilee, we knew we would be seeing it many more times over the course of our journey. The small four-table restaurant definitely lived up to its reputation. The redbelly tilapia smothered with spices was cooked over an open fire. We all concurred that it tasted very similar to red snapper. Rounding out our meal were generous portions of hummus made from garbanzo beans. Plenty of *falafel* was on hand; these delicious chickpea fritters are Israel's national dish and can be found on practically every street corner. Dessert was *ma'aroud,* rolled cookies stuffed with dates. It was soon time to head out. Next stop, the Dead Sea.

DEAD SEA

Thankfully, after this magnificent meal, we had a couple of hours to relax in the car while we drove south. About 90 miles later, the famous body of water came into view. The Sea of Salt is the lowest point on earth. It is called the Dead Sea because no fish can survive in its salty water. The stunning landscape of the Negev Desert and Judean Mountains surround this beautiful, blue basin. The only major source flowing into the Dead Sea is the Jordan River; there are no outlet streams.

The Dead Sea was an important trade route in ancient times. Herod the Great built several palaces on the western bank. The most famous of these, Masada, is another great attraction in the area. This ancient fortress was a refuge in AD 70 for a small group of zealots escaping persecution by the Romans. Today, you can climb the steep incline or take a cable car up to Masada. Some archeologists believe the towns of Sodom and Gomorrah lie beneath the Dead Sea or in the vicinity.

In the 1940s and 1950s, hundreds of religious documents were found in 12 caves near the settlement of Qumran. These Dead Sea Scrolls found by Bedouins and later, archeologists, have great historic and religious significance because they include the second-oldest manuscripts that are written in the Hebrew Bible.

Looking across the Dead Sea, Tommy had many visions from the Lord. With great concern, he began sharing these visions.

Tommy

"A lot of people may not be able to understand this vision. The Dead Sea area threw me for a shock. I saw Mount Pisgah and could understand how Moses looked out at the Promised Land. There are three springs coming out of Mount Pisgah. Two things associated with the spiritual world are fire and water, but most people don't want the fire. The Dead Sea looks as good as the Sea of Galilee, but it's dead. There's plenty of life flowing into the Dead Sea from the Jordan River, but none goes out.

It's the way most churches are today. Mainstream churches are dead; some segments of those churches are alive. I am not talking about the remnant who follow God. The church, in general, is lost. Some of the doctrines taught are dead; they aren't correct. The saints talked about the Shekinah Glory. I want the supernatural, like they did. Signs and wonders. That's what happened at Azusa. I want everything God has; I want the Shekinah Glory.

I didn't much like what I saw at the Dead Sea, and was a little nervous. I didn't want to go down to the water. I kept trying to look away, but God made me look at the sea. I saw lewdness, nakedness, and sin; it was the church. The church is primarily backslidden; ask God which ones. So many are too proud of their denominations. I saw the pride of a lot of the churches at the Dead Sea.

God is giving us another chance though. I don't want to tear down the church, but build it up. I love truth. Don't compromise, but watch how you say things. There will be a great falling away from the Word of God. Jesus said you take your philosophy and make the Word of God to no effect, and that's what the church is doing today.

Our country needs a good cleansing. The United States is in trouble; we need to keep praying and seeking God. We need a great awakening. Other countries have had it; Azusa was an awakening. We need one now! We have watered down the Word of God so much, that it's nothing anymore. If it clashes with the Word of God, you can take all the philosophies and throw them away; I'm going with the Word of God.

Whatever God wants to do is fine with me. God also showed me that a revival is coming. It is happening all over the world, including all of Israel. Everything has a purpose and significance, including the Dead Sea. God is going to wake up the church! However, I don't think we can attain the level of success others achieved without the corresponding sacrifice. All the military bunkers around this area were not torn down. These will be used for camping when the revival starts!"

⊱⊰

After a very busy, but thrilling, day, we headed back to the hotel for the evening. To make our time on the drive pass more quickly, Tommy told us many stories that had been revealed to him by the Azusa Street saints.

AZUSA

Sister Langtroff

"Sister Laura Langtroff, at age 16, became part of the Azusa Revival when her friend, Sister Lucille, invited her to attend a meeting. She moved to Pisgah in 1955, and I met her when she was in her 70s. She stood about 5' 7" tall and had long, dark hair which she kept up in a glory bun. Sister Laura was from a very well-to-do family and was wealthy in her own right. However, she chose to live at Pisgah with her Azusa friends.

Sister Laura told me that she went to the meeting every night, and she participated in at least three or four miracles each night. One very memorable miracle concerned a little boy, about 10 years old, who was possessed by demons. His family kept him strapped down in a wheelchair because he was very violent and hard to control. The poor child would hiss and foam at the mouth; it was pitiful. Sister Laura got excited. "This is going to be fun!" she said. She began talking to the demon, until somebody finally rebuked her. "Laura, you need to do what you're supposed to do. Stop playing." She quickly grabbed the boy by his head and took authority, commanding the demon to come out! The demon said it would come out, and it did.

Unfortunately, the boy did not get better. Laura realized he was possessed by multiple demons. She spent the next hour casting out one demon after another, until nothing came out of the boy's mouth. She asked the boy his name and if he was free of demons. He told her his name and said that, yes, he was free. Sister Laura explained to the boy that his house was clean, but those demons will come back with seven times more just like them or worse. She laid hands on him, prayed, and commanded him to receive the baptism of the Holy Spirit. He started speaking in tongues. Glory to God!

One of the most amazing miracles Sister Laura was thrilled to be part of involved a woman who came to a meeting carrying a staff. She looked like a skeleton and could barely breathe; she was dying of lung cancer. She lived about two miles from the Azusa mission. She started walking there at three o'clock in the afternoon, but didn't arrive until six in the evening. She literally took one baby step at a time, placing the staff in front of her, then scooting her feet up to it. She repeated this slow process for three hours until she got to the revival. At the time, a service wasn't going on in the church, but someone was always there. And God was always moving.

She entered the warehouse and looked around, her eyes landing on Sister Laura. "That's the woman I want to pray for me," she said. After Sister Laura asked her what she could do for her, the lady replied, "I won't live through the night if God doesn't heal me; I'll die. Doctors say my lungs are ate up with cancer, and I can hardly breathe. I've been losing weight for about a year." The feeble woman was about 5' 6" tall and weighed 65 pounds. She was skin and bones. Sister Laura laid hands on her and prayed for her. Immediately, she started breathing normally! For the next three hours, she gained 40 pounds while basking in the Shekinah Glory. She ate nothing. She yelled, "My lungs are not hurting; I can breathe like when I was young!"

Talk about a celebration! Sister Laura was a shouter. In her excitement while praising God, her glory bun shook loose and hairpins went flying. But the story just gets better.

The next day, the lady visited her doctor, Thomas Wyatt. He did not recognize her at all. When she told him who she was, he could not believe his eyes. He ran some tests and pronounced her cancer-free. He told her it was impossible for her to gain that much weight back in a few days. She said yes it was impossible for her to do that, but God sure could. "You're going down to that warehouse, aren't you?" he asked. He had been losing all his patients to Azusa Street! It was about to shut down his clinic.

After confirmation that she was, he started attending meetings at Azusa Street with her. In a few months, he had given up his traditional doctor's practice. Dr. Wyatt founded "Wings of Healing" and witnessed many miracles through his ministry. Now, hold on! The story gets even better!

In 2007, after the release of my first book, I received a phone call from a lady. She proceeded to tell me that the lady who walked to Azusa with the staff was her grandmother. I was amazed! She continued, "We used to ask my grandmother to sit down at our dinners and tell us about her miracle at Azusa Street. Some people are trying to say that Dr. Wyatt wasn't really at Azusa. People are trying to discredit the story. Don't let them kid you, Tommy. Don't believe them." Crying, she said, "My married name is Wyatt, I married Dr. Thomas Wyatt's grandson. Thomas Wyatt was my grandmother's doctor." How about that! Came full circle. What an ending to that story!

Brother and Sister Lankford

When I was at Pisgah, I had the privilege of getting to know Brother and Sister Lankford. I would enjoy strawberry ice cream with them while they told me some amazing miracles that happened at the mission. The Lankfords were always thrilled to be used by God to bring about healings and miracles. At Azusa, they were 20 and 18 years old. Brother Lankford told me about a man whose fingers were caught in a machine at work. It ripped off two fingers! The man had heard that unbelievable miracles had been taking place at a warehouse on Azusa Street. In pain and with the expectation of being healed, he came to the mission.

Upon entering, he encountered Brother and Sister Lankford. Inquiring about how they could pray for him, the man explained what had happened. "Let's ask God to grow them out," said Brother Lankford. He grabbed the man's hand and held it high in the air; Sister Lankford helped by holding up the man's arm. As Brother Lankford began to pray, the man's fingers began to grow out! Even his fingernails grew in. Sister Lankford fainted at the sight of such a miracle. He and the man started rejoicing and showing everyone what happened. "These weren't here before. Look, God grew these fingers out!"

Brother Lankford went on to tell about a man with a horrible tumor on his spine. The outline of the tumor showed underneath the man's shirt. It stood out three inches, and was about a foot long and four inches wide. The man was middle-aged and had the affliction for around three years. He was scheduled for x-rays the next day to determine what the tumor was. Brother Lankford prayed for his healing; the tumor sank into the man's body and disappeared. The man was totally healed!"

<hr />

The power of the early Church was that they put God first. Today, many church members put themselves first. The Church exerts little influence on the world. In many ways, it has become backslidden and powerless. The Church needs to return to the faith once delivered to the saints. Revival—when God invades humankind with supernatural solutions—is the method by which His Church will be transformed! When we go to the threshing floor, God will deal with us, burning away all chaff. The river of mercy, obedience, and joy will once again flow through us. When the Holy Spirit touches us, we will gladly turn a new page and start a wonderful new chapter.

Whoever believes in me, as Scripture has said, rivers of living water will flow from within them (John 7:38 NIV).

And the border shall go down to the Jordan, and its limit shall be the Salt Sea. This shall be your land as defined by its borders all around (Numbers 34:12 ESV).

And Jesus, walking by the Sea of Galilee, saw two brothers, Simon called Peter and Andrew his brother, casting a net into the sea; for they were fishermen (Matthew 4:18 NKJV).

We have not repented and interceded enough until the pain and sorrow, the very burden of our families, our tribes, and our nations, become our very own.

—BISHOP ARMSTRONG CHEGGEH

If we wept as much in the prayer closet as devout Jews have done at the Wailing Wall in Jerusalem, we would now be enjoying a prevailing, purging revival!

—LEONARD RAVENHILL

9

Glory

*The Lord said to him: "I have heard the prayer and
plea you have made before me; I have consecrated this
temple, which you have built, by putting my Name there
forever. My eyes and my heart will always be there"*
(1 KINGS 9:3 NIV).

The old man wiped tears from his face. It had been a long and
hard journey to this day. Torture, starvation, mass shootings, gas
chambers, diseases, death marches. The horror of it was indescribable. He had spent years in Auschwitz watching thousands
die and wondering why he was alive. All his family had been
lost to the evils of the Shoah. This destruction of God's chosen
people had finally come to an end.

Leaving war-torn Europe, Eli felt privileged to emigrate
to Zion in 1948. He felt proud being one of the early settlers,

and thrilled when Israel once more became a nation. God had ordained it long ago, and He had kept His word. Life had been tough, but Eli had farmed the little patch of land granted to him by the government. He made a decent living. But for the past 19 years, Eli had been forbidden to be in the eastern part of Jerusalem. However, the day had finally arrived for that to change. Israel had prevailed. The old man fell to his knees, bowed his head to the Almighty, and touched the Western Wall.

⊷⊶

Throngs of people swarmed around us as we sipped our cool lemonade. Local residents, along with a river of tourists from around the globe, made their way to the mighty Western Wall. Security was tight; soldiers patrolled the grounds. The sounds of prayers uttered aloud drifted through the air. The stifling heat permeated the ancient stones and radiated throughout the crowd. Music and singing could be heard in various pockets of the plaza. At most times of the day, the wall is lined with people deep in prayers. A chorus of Hebrew emanated from around the wall.

The Western Wall is a place of pilgrimage and prayer for the Jewish people. These remains are the western support wall of the Temple Mount. The wall is sacred because it is considered to be holy ground due to the proximity of the Holy of Holies. King Herod built the wall as an expansion of the Second Temple. The First Temple, built by King Solomon, was destroyed by the Babylonians in 587 BC, and the Second Temple was destroyed by the Romans in AD 70. Tradition, archeological research, and history have authenticated the Western Wall. This famous wall is about 160 feet long and 60 feet high. Many Jews still pray toward the Temple Mount.

Praying for Jerusalem is one way to bless Israel. The Bible promises that if we bless Israel, we will be blessed. The Western Wall is the place where we can feel our Christian faith intertwine with Jewish faith so strongly. Praying there is like touching the hope of Jewish people. You can feel the stones worn smooth by so many others before you, reaching out in longing and prayer.

Finishing our drinks, we made our way down to the Prayer Plaza. This plaza is actually an outdoor synagogue, holding up to 60,000 people. The rabbis believe that the divine presence never departs from the Western Wall. Thousands of people visit the wall every year to offer prayers. There is a custom of pushing slips of paper with prayers on them into the wall's cracks. Hyssop grew out of many cracks, emanating a lovely mint smell. In the Bible, hyssop was used in cleansing rituals and symbolically as cleansing the soul.

As we were talking and praying in the plaza, an elderly lady came up to us. She spoke only Arabic, no English. She was dressed in a flowery skirt with a silk scarf covering her head, a large cross dangling from her neck. The woman pantomimed that she wanted to pray for Tommy, who was seated in a wheelchair. Appreciative of her request, we nodded yes. Beautiful words to God were spoken in this foreign tongue, no doubt beseeching the Almighty for health and happiness for Tommy. "Although I had no idea what she said, she reminded me of Anna in the Bible. This was all from God," said Tommy. Anna was a prophet who never left the temple, but worshipped day and night, fasting and praying (see Luke 2:36-38).

This touching moment reassured us that in spite of all our differences, Christians all over the world can agree on many things—revival, love for others, and the much-anticipated return of our Savior! The wall is divided into two sections, one for men and one for women. Tommy, Daniel, and Clif went one way; I went another. Because I had been to the wall several times, I remained in an area where I could observe Tommy's first visit. What an honor to witness this momentous event; I thanked God for the opportunity. Reverence lined Tommy's face as he prayed deeply for the nation of Israel.

Tommy

"When I walked down the cobbled stairs, I could see that many people there were Christians. I believe most of the Israelis know that Christians support them. We pray for Israel and back Israel. As I was praying, a tiny sparrow landed on a nearby twig and started singing right to me. It really warmed my heart. It seemed as if he was singing peace, peace, peace. One of the visions I saw that day involved many soldiers, big guns, and some battles at the Western Wall. Israel will win every time. I'm not sure what it means, but they were there.

Israel will always have problems until Jesus takes over. Also, I saw an angel over every single person who was there praying. There was a Jewish man sitting there, reading the Torah in his lap. An angel was right behind him. The man looked up and smiled at me; he will fit in somehow with prophecy. People ask me why God lets me see things like this, and I say, I don't know, ask God. I think the same thing myself."

When Tommy finished his prayer and backed away from the wall, the men met me in the plaza. Tommy had a delightful smile on his face. He told us about the cheerful bird, saying it reminded him of Brother Anderson, one of the Azusa Street saints who was always so full of joy.

AZUSA

Brother Anderson

"Brother Anderson was only 15 years old when the Azusa Street Revival began. He was one of the first ones at the mission to receive the baptism of the Holy Spirit and speak in tongues. The others at the old warehouse called him a modern-day Zacchaeus because he liked to climb on the benches to get a better view of the miracles going on. Zacchaeus climbed a sycamore tree to get a better view of Jesus.

I met Brother Anderson at Pisgah. He had slicked-back, gray hair and was balding. His complexion was ruddy, and his eyes twinkled. He seemed to be happy and full of life, always walking with a spring in his step. In all the years I knew him, never once did I see him frown. When Brother Anderson would tell stories about Azusa Street, he sat on the edge of his rocking chair. His excitement was contagious! The passing decades never dulled the thrill of what took place at Azusa Street. He lived frugally; gold could never buy what he possessed—priceless memories and miraculous experiences.

The Shekinah Glory was an endless source of wonder for young Anderson, as well as all the other saints. He said it could be described, but not understood. Inside the building, there would be a glow. The mist would often get so thick, it would fill the entire building. When God began working miracles, the mist would glow even brighter. Anderson said it was like a part of Heaven had come down.

After about ten times attending services at the mission, God started using Brother Anderson to assist Him in healing people. He was part of many healings of folks who were blind or deaf. One of his favorite stories involved a woman named Diane. Diane lived about a half mile away from 312 Azusa Street. She was the first person, but by no means the last, to call the fire department because she believed the mission was on fire. She saw fire shooting 50 feet off the top of the building and a ball of fire about 100 feet above it shooting flames down, meeting the flame coming off the building. The fire department responded that night and a few other nights.

They finally realized that it was a supernatural fire sent by God, and the building was never on fire. When others would report the fire, they explained it was God and not to worry. Brother Anderson said it was an amazing thing to witness; he could then understand about Moses and the burning bush. The more people worshipped in tongues, the greater the flames.

Diane was a young woman in the early 1900s. However, I actually got to meet her at Pisgah when she was long into retirement age. It was wonderful to hear the story from both points of view—the man who prayed and the woman who was healed.

Back in the day, Diane had a large tumor on the side of her head; it was the size of half of a basketball. When she walked, she would have to carry it in her hand because it was so heavy and awkward. It was inoperable back then. Nowadays, surgeons could have removed it. The tumor had progressed into being malignant; Diane was given a short time to live.

One evening, at her wit's end, she decided to walk to the mission. She had heard that miracles were taking place there. It was her last hope. "I thought to myself, *What have I got to lose? I'm dying, and if I go there and I die, so what? The doctors can't do anything. The tumor is too big to cut off.* I took a pain pill and got ready. Although the tumor was extremely painful, I waddled with my kids down to Azusa, holding that growth in my hand," Diane said.

Upon entering the mission, Brother Anderson spotted her. He leapt down from the bench he was standing on and told Diane that God was going to work a miracle for her. She rolled her eyes and said she came to Azusa for exactly that. Brother Anderson and others laid hands on her and began praying. Immediately the tumor began shrinking, then disappeared within two minutes! Shocked beyond belief, Diane yelled, "I'm healed!"

That miracle saved her life. In 1914, God instructed her to start a ministry—a soup kitchen for the needy. "I looked in my purse and told God that I only had a quarter. He said that was sufficient. So, I took that 25 cents and went to the farmers' market, buying as many vegetables as I could. Then I made soup," said Diane. That humble beginning on skid row progressed into a massive feeding program, serving thousands of meals daily. When I met Diane in the 1960s, she was still serving food to the downtrodden. She had been honored several times by the governor of California and other officials.

Brother Anderson was fascinated by William Seymour. He used to sit as near as he could when Seymour would sit with the box over his head. He wondered if he was praying under it, but could never see for sure. Brother Anderson said that Seymour was a man of strong faith and tremendous wisdom. Every time

Seymour said something, it would happen. He witnessed miracles through Seymour that were too numerous to count. Several times, Brother Seymour would point to about a dozen people who suffered from rheumatoid arthritis or another ailment and tell them that within a few minutes they would be healed. It came to pass every single time!

One of the healings Brother Anderson saw was when a man came in with a deformed face with small growths all over it. These things caused him to look extremely ugly. Seymour prayed for the man; immediately the growths fell off, restoring his face to normal. Mission volunteers cleaned up the hideous growths that had fallen to the floor.

Brother Anderson confirmed what some of the other saints told me. The amazing gifts of God, such as the power to heal, stayed with Brother Seymour as long as he continued to put the box over his head during the services. After a few years, when he stopped putting the box over his head, the gifts disappeared."

⊷✦⊶

It had been another incredible day in Jerusalem. Everywhere we went, it seemed like we were standing on holy ground. It was a privilege to worship at this ancient wall of Solomon. As evening approached, the music of the city filled our ears. We are blessed to be able to sing praises and to worship the Creator of the universe. The destiny of nations is affected by worship. Our lives should be ones of continual worship, honoring the Almighty God with how we think, act, and live.

When all the Israelites saw the fire coming down and the glory of the Lord above the temple, they knelt on the pavement with their faces to the ground, and they worshiped and gave thanks to the Lord, saying, "He is good; his love endures forever" (2 Chronicles 7:3 NIV).

"Go up into the mountains and bring down timber and build my house, so that I may take pleasure in it and be honored," says the Lord (Haggai 1:8 NIV).

Therefore this is what the Lord says: "I will return to Jerusalem with mercy, and there my house will be rebuilt. And the measuring line will be stretched out over Jerusalem," declares the Lord Almighty (Zechariah 1:16 NIV).

A man's desperation for the things of God should melt away all preoccupations with self, notoriety, public image and social status. Your hunger and thirst, if it is genuine, will drive you to eat and to drink regardless of the opinions of others. You will be willing to be a fool in the sight of others, in order to be embraced in the arms of the Lord.

—STEVE HILL

God loves with a great love the man whose heart is bursting with a passion for the impossible.

—WILLIAM BOOTH

10

I Don't Know, Ask God

Old City

*I will give one tribe to his son so that David my
servant may always have a lamp before me in
Jerusalem, the city where I chose to put my Name*
(1 KINGS 11:36 NIV).

Simon was in the wrong place at the right time. Visiting Jerusalem for Passover had been a long-awaited dream of his. The journey from Cyrene had taken several weeks. It would have been a perfect celebration if not for the Romans patrolling all the streets day and night. But at least he was in the holy city. He awoke early and enjoyed a hearty breakfast before heading to the Cyrenian synagogue to worship. Along the way, Simon heard a commotion and saw throngs of people scurrying out of the way of Roman soldiers. Curious, he stopped to see what it was all about.

A criminal was being herded along the street, being whipped by the cruel soldiers. The Man was bleeding and struggling to carry a heavy wooden cross. Simon was repulsed by the sight of the Man heading to His crucifixion. *A disgusting punishment no matter how horrible the crime,* he thought. Suddenly, one of the Roman guards grabbed his arm and forced him into the path. Simon was more outraged than scared. The soldier told him to carry the cross for the criminal. He refused. But only once. It took only the threat of the whip to convince him to help.

Shouldering the massive cross, he began the tortuous journey to a place called Golgotha. The walk was difficult for him, but even more so for the Man beside him. Blood poured from His open wounds. Walking was hard enough; talking was out of the question. Along the way, some people were jeering, calling the Man, "King of the Jews." A few were weeping. The more Simon tried to hate the Man, the more compassion arose inside him. *Something is happening to me that I can't explain,* he thought. As the long walk progressed, Simon became stronger; the cross no longer seemed heavy. He became convinced that this Man was not a criminal, not even an average man... but oh so much more.

The journey up the mountain ended. His task was finished, but the Man beside him had an arduous road ahead. How would He be able to withstand the agony and pain? What had begun in disgust and anger had ended in honor and reverence. Looking into the face of the Man destined to die, he nodded his head. What a privilege to carry this small burden for this Man—this Son of God, Jesus.

‹·§·›

Rising early so as not to waste a moment, we headed into the Old City. The sun shone brightly as we walked the already busy streets. Chattering voices filled the air, no doubt haggling over the various wares for sale. The aroma of the world's most delicious coffee wafted through the breeze. The slick stones showed wear from millions of pilgrims who had tread upon them. In these ancient streets, you are truly transported back 2,000 years ago.

During its long history, Jerusalem has been attacked 52 times, captured and recaptured 44 times, and destroyed twice. The Old City was settled 4,000 years before the birth of Christ, making Jerusalem one of the oldest cities in the world. The Old City is divided into four uneven sectors—the Jewish, Christian, Muslim, and Armenian Quarters. The whole area is only about one-third of a square mile in size.

JEWISH QUARTER

We began our visit in the Jewish Quarter, home of the Western Wall and the Temple Mount. The Western Wall is the last remnant of the temples built by Solomon and King Herod. The Jewish faithful go here to pray. Also in this area is the Temple Mount.

The Mount of the House of God is a flat plaza surrounded by retaining walls. Jews turn toward the Temple Mount when they pray, since it is the holiest site in Judaism. Many Jews will not walk on the Mount due to its extreme sanctity; they do not want to accidentally enter the area where the Holy of Holies once stood. Some aspect of the Divine Presence is still on the site, according to Rabbinical law. Judaism teaches that this is the place where God gathered the dust to create Adam. Other important biblical events were said to take place here—the binding of Isaac, Jacob's dream, the prayer of Isaac and Rebekah, and the location of the threshing floor purchased by David.

In 1948, all Jewish residents were evicted from the Old City when Jordan captured it. However, Israeli forces recaptured East Jerusalem in 1967 and reunited it with the western part of the city. In the 1970s, the Jewish Quarter was rebuilt, allowing about 2,000 Jews to return to the Old City to live. Meandering through the winding streets was like stepping back in time. It's a lovely area and very well kept. One of the most beautiful sites in this area is a huge menorah made with 95 pounds of 24-karat gold. This seven-branched candelabrum is a replica of the menorah that was used in the First and Second Temples.

The Levitical priests lit the menorah in the sanctuary every evening, then cleaned it out every morning, replacing the old wicks with new ones. This spectacular replica is displayed in a transparent case, overlooking the stairs that lead down to the Western Wall plaza and the Temple Mount. The menorah is a unique Jewish symbol bringing light into the world.

Tommy said, "I wouldn't mind being one of those priests carrying that menorah into the temple when it is built. You know the end-times are getting close. They are starting to replicate a lot of things that go into the Third Temple. God gave me a vision about this very thing. When our guide, Daniel, told me what the menorah was for, I suddenly saw two priests in white robes; both of them came up and held the menorah high. I could see them following a man inside. I assumed it was Jesus, although I couldn't see His face. That really meant a lot to me."

Make a lampstand of pure gold. Hammer out its base and shaft, and make its flowerlike cups, buds and blossoms of one piece with them. Six branches are to extend from the sides of the lampstand—three on one side and three on the other. Three cups shaped like almond flowers with buds and blossoms are to be on one branch, three on the next branch, and the same for all six branches extending from the lampstand (Exodus 25:31-33 NIV).

MUSLIM QUARTER

Next on our agenda was the Muslim Quarter, in the northeast section of the Old City. This larger area is dominated by the Dome of the Rock, a shrine where Abraham was going to sacrifice Isaac, but his hand was stayed by God. This beautiful site should not be missed; the massive dome is covered in shiny brass.

"Mount Moriah was a big surprise to me, how straight up it is. It's the gateway to Heaven," said Tommy.

The lure of the huge souk between the two quarters was too strong to resist. We were ready to test our negotiating skills since the vendors actually expect you to haggle with them. The bazaar is filled with religious items, souvenirs, pottery, jewelry, textiles and just about everything else you can think of. One of my favorite things are all the beautiful woven scarves of every color imaginable. A delicious and healthy treat of pomegranate juice is available around every turn. The mesmerizing scent of hundreds of spices wafts through the air. All kinds of food are offered for your eating pleasure: looking and tasting incredible.

There are so many alleyways; it is easy to get lost or turned around. While there, a man with a cart loaded with fruit and vegetables had an accident. His cart turned over, spilling produce, cups, and napkins everywhere. As he hurriedly picked up the mess, dozens of people yelled at him as they passed; never stopping to help. We must always be willing to help others, not just fellow believers.

Scripture is full of God's command to His people to do so. It's a holy thing to do; it is a way that the Lord sets apart His Church from the world. Galatians 6:2 (NIV) tells us, *"Carry each other's burdens, and in this way you will fulfill the law of Christ."* We took a few moments to help this elderly gentleman right his cart and stack his produce back upon it. He was very appreciative and thanked us profusely.

A couple hours and two dozen scarves later, it was time to head to our next stop. We got through without damaging our bank accounts too badly, but we had to buy extra suitcases to transport our finds home! We considered it a contribution to the local economy. We could have stayed in the Muslim Quarter shopping for hours. But, it was time to leave. Clif had an appointment in the Christian Quarter.

CHRISTIAN QUARTER

The most exquisite place in the Christian Quarter is the Church of the Holy Sepulchre. It is identified as the place of the crucifixion of Jesus and, also His empty tomb. These are considered to be the two holiest sites in Christianity.

In AD 312, after seeing a vision of a cross in the sky, Constantine the Great converted to Christianity. He legalized the religion and sent his mother, Helena, to Jerusalem to look for Jesus's burial place. Three crosses were found near a tomb, leading Helena and the bishops to believe they had found Calvary. Constantine had the Church of the Holy Sepulchre built there.

At one time, the whole complex was richly decorated, according to a biographer of Constantine's. This spectacular church is filled with soaring columns and hundreds of arched windows and doorways, topped by a huge, blue dome 65 feet up. Today, gorgeous murals and mosaics fill the walls. There are so many areas to explore in the church. Included are several chapels—two underground, the Stone of the Anointing, the Rock of Calvary, and the Tomb of Christ. This tomb is one of two places that locals say could be the actual tomb of our Lord. No one really knows. All are breathtaking and extremely moving.

It was time for Clif's appointment. Winding our way through the alleys, we found Razzouk Tattoo. This shop has been in existence since AD 1300! Wassim, the current owner, is the 27th generation of the family practicing the art of tattoo on visitors to the Old City. Wassim told us, "Tattooing is an art that the Razzouk family brought with them five centuries ago from Egypt. They had already been practicing the art in Egypt for 700 years. Our ancestors used tattoos to mark Christian Copts in Egypt with a small cross on the inside of the wrist to grant them access to churches; those without it would have difficulty entering. In this country, many tattoo artists learned the skill from my grandfather, Jacob. Our ancestors from Egypt brought with them the wooden hand-carved stamps that act as stencils for the religious designs based on Bible motifs. For example, the crucifixion, the ascension, the Madonna, and more. Pilgrims would stand in line waiting for their turn to be tattooed with either a cross or another design as certification of their pilgrimage or as a souvenir."

Clif knew exactly what he wanted—a cross. This design consisted of a large cross with symbols in each quadrant. They stand for Jesus Christ Alpha Omega. This was a replica of the cross discovered inside the tomb near the Garden of Gethsemane.

Leaving the busy shop of Razzouk, we stopped for some amazing Israeli coffee at a shop called Aroma. We decided it was hands-down the best coffee we had ever tasted! Rich, dark, and aromatic, it soon became a "can't do without" item on our daily agenda. Throughout this Quarter, nativities carved from olive wood are abundant. These beautiful carvings range from very small to extremely large, relatively cheap to outrageously expensive. In addition to nativities, other biblical scenes can be had—The Last Supper, Jesus on the Cross, Jesus Washing His Disciples' Feet, and more.

ARMENIAN QUARTER

Our final stop on this busy day was the Armenian Quarter, the smallest of the four areas. The Armenian presence in Jerusalem dates to the 4th century AD. At that time, Armenia adopted Christianity as a national religion; monks settled in Jerusalem. Today, around 2,000 Armenians live in Jerusalem, mostly in this Quarter. The Armenian sector is dominated by a beautiful, domed basilica completed in the 12th century near the Zion Gate. The church is dedicated to James, one of the 12 apostles of Jesus, and James, the brother of Jesus. Exquisite metalwork, a soaring dome, and fantastic artwork decorate this lovely cathedral. We enjoyed a delicious meal at a restaurant that is literally built into the inner wall of Old Jerusalem. After filling up on hummus, pita bread, and lamb kabobs, we enjoyed strolling through the Quarter and looking at the intricate Armenian ceramics.

Heading back to our hotel during rush hour, we had plenty of time to convince Tommy to tell us more Azusa Street stories. He was always happy to oblige with the tales from these dear saints.

Azusa

Sister Dundee

"Sister Dundee was close to 80 years old when I met her. She had been around Pisgah since the years of Dr. Yoakum. Italian by birth, her hair was still black with a bit of gray. She always wore it in a glory bun. Her gold-rimmed glasses were usually perched at the end of her nose. She wore those granny boots with hooks and eyelets, just like Sister Carney did. She had experienced all kinds of miracles at Azusa. A quiet lady by nature, I would have to coax the stories from her.

One that she told me was about a little boy, about 6 years old, who had to have his head and body strapped to a wheelchair. Sister Dundee went over to his parents and asked what was wrong with the little fella. All they knew was he had some kind of paralysis, but could breathe okay. She told them, "Well this is good, for the Lord's name will be glorified, but we can't just pray for him and leave him tied up here." She undid the strap on his neck and told his parents to hold up his body. "In the name of Jesus Christ, be made perfectly whole," she prayed. Immediately the boy jerked and wanted to get down and play. "Tommy, I no more had gotten out 'in the name of Jesus,' and he was healed!" Sister Dundee said she got to see this little boy quite a bit over the next four years.

Let me tell you another story that I have never told before. There was a grandma, not real old. She waddled like a duck. Her legs were twisted, her back and hips were a mess. She came to the Azusa mission. Sister Dundee usually prayed for children, so she noticed the woman when she came in with a bunch of kids. "These kids aren't yours, are they?" she asked the lady. The lady explained that no, these were her grandchildren, but she took care of them.

Sister Dundee asked if it was hard to take care of them since she was in such bad condition. The woman said, "Well, isn't God doing miracles here?" Sister Dundee said, "Yes, let's see what God will do with you. "She laid hands on her and prayed for her. Before their eyes, this woman's hips, back, and twisted legs began popping. You could hear it happening. She straightened up and was instantly healed. You see, at Azusa Street, things happened fast! She was old when she went to Azusa, so I never got to meet her, but I did get to meet some of her grandkids. They said that their grandma was so pathetic, she could hardly walk. She mainly told her grandkids what to do. After her healing, she was peppy and could work circles around them, they said."

⊰✦⊱

It had been another marvelous day in Jerusalem. History had come alive! What a blessing to experience it.

Pray for the peace of Jerusalem: May those who love you be secure (Psalm 122:6 NIV).

At that time they will call Jerusalem The Throne of the Lord, and all nations will gather in Jerusalem to honor the name of the Lord. No longer will they follow the stubbornness of their evil hearts (Jeremiah 3:17 NIV).

May it please you to prosper Zion, to build up the walls of Jerusalem (Psalm 51:18 NIV).

Moves of God must have the cross as the central point to maintain their genuineness—keeping first things first. The throne is the center of His kingdom, and on His throne sits the Lamb of God. The blood sacrifice will be honored and celebrated throughout eternity. While it is the resurrection that correctly illustrates and empowers the Christian life, it is the cross that bring us there. There is no resurrection without the cross.

—BILL JOHNSON

Christ the Lord is risen today. Sons of men and angels say. Raise your joys and triumphs high: Sing, ye heavens, and earth reply.

—CHARLES WESLEY

11

The Secret Is the Anointing

Golgotha and Garden Tomb

Blessed and holy are those who share in the first
resurrection. The second death has no power over
them, but they will be priests of God and of Christ
and will reign with him for a thousand years
(REVELATION 20:6 NIV).

The woman walked through the peaceful garden reminiscing about the last few years, especially the last few days. She thought about the trials and tribulations she and her fellow believers had been through. But she also remembered the joy and laughter. What an honor it had been learning at the feet of Jesus. He had come to save the world; He had absolutely saved her. Tears ran down her lovely face as she thought about the agony her dear friend had suffered. How brave He had been; how generous to the very end…

asking God to forgive His tormentors and executioners. The least she could do was visit His resting place every day and pray. It was a beautiful garden—olive trees, birds, flowers. Bracing herself as the sadness swept over her, Mary fell to her knees when she saw the tomb. The huge rock had been rolled away!

❧

The resurrection is what empowers the Christian faith. However, the cross had to come first. The purpose of Jesus coming to this world was to die upon the cross as a sacrifice for humankind's sins. All of Scripture leads up to this pinnacle moment in the history of humanity.

While there is no consensus as to the location of the crucifixion site, we visited one of the two most often regarded as possibilities. John 19:20 says the site was *"near the city,"* while Hebrews 13:12 says it was *"outside the city gate."* Matthew and Mark both explained that the site was accessible to "passersby." So the location would have been outside a major gate where people could see Jesus being crucified.

GOLGOTHA

In all four Gospels, the site is called Golgotha, a skull-shaped hill in Jerusalem. In ancient texts, Golgotha was said to be a hill resembling a skullcap, not the face of a skull. It was not far from the tomb in which our Savior could have been buried. As previously mentioned, many scholars say it is the spot now covered by the Church of the Holy Sepulchre or a hill called Gordon's Calvary, north of the Damascus Gate.

Like so many of the places we visited in Israel, the exact location is unknown. However, it is a moving experience just to be in the vicinity. What a feeling of awe and reverence! For a few moments, the four of us just stared at Golgotha. We thanked our Father for sending His precious Son to offer us salvation. The magnitude of what happened there was overwhelming!

Garden Tomb

Nearby is a garden where many Christians go to visit an ancient Jewish tomb. Some scholars believe this Garden Tomb could be the site of Christ's burial and resurrection. It is located just outside the Old City walls. In John 19:41 (NIV), the Bible says there was a garden near the place where Jesus was crucified, and *"in the garden a new tomb, in which no one had ever been laid."* The question of the exact location of Jesus's tomb is a contentious subject. Again, many believe it is in the Church of the Holy Sepulchre, while others insist it is the Garden Tomb.

Going into the tomb was a somber experience. The tomb has two chambers with stone benches along the back wall of the first chamber and along the sides of the walls of the second chamber. Painted on the wall inside the Garden Tomb is a beautiful cross. In the quadrants of the cross are symbols for Jesus Christ Alpha Omega. You will recall that Clif had this exact cross tattooed on his arm in the Old City.

"I could envision Jesus's body lying there. The sadness caused me to shake nervously. However, the resurrection anointing is still there. I know that revival will soon break loose in Jerusalem and all over the world. It's not up to us—it's up to God," said Tommy.

While walking through this beautiful garden, we had ample opportunity to contemplate those events of long ago. Especially the resurrection. Can you imagine what the women at the tomb

The River of Zion

felt like when the angel told them that Jesus was not there, but risen? The stone had been rolled away from the tomb! As believers, we need to seek the living God and find our purpose in this life. We need to lift our hands and worship Him in spirit and in truth. What an astounding event that took place around 2,000 years ago. God saved the world!

Whether or not this is the exact location of the crucifixion and the resurrection is ultimately unimportant. What is truly important is that people have an encounter with the living Messiah today.

While we were cooling off under a lovely shade tree, Tommy shared several stories from the Azusa Street saints.

AZUSA

Brother David Garcia

"The Apostolic Faith Mission on Azusa Street was the first totally integrated church in America. People of all races worshipped together. When William Seymour came down to the meeting, he made sure all groups were blended together. David Garcia was a young Mexican-American who attended services there every evening after work, as well as every weekend. I met Brother David at Pisgah; he had lived there since around 1955. He was about 5' 7" inches tall and weighed about 200 pounds. In 1906, Brother David was about 18 years old. He lived almost a mile from the old warehouse. At Pisgah, when we got together, he would serve strong coffee to me. No cookies and milk in that house!

One of the best stories Brother David ever told me was about a nearby train station. One evening he ran to Azusa Street to find Frank Bartleman. When he found him, Brother

148

David was out of breath and hurriedly told Bartleman that he needed to follow him to the train station about a half mile away. He said, "You've got to come and see this! The anointing is far beyond where it has been in the past!" Bartleman had previously talked about a circle of blood, blocks around the Azusa warehouse, where the power of God extended outward. When they got to the station, they witnessed people getting off the train, walking across the platform, and falling out in the Spirit, often speaking in tongues. Someone told them that it had been happening all day.

Brother David said the greatest miracle he had been involved in was multiple healings of two women and a man who all had crippling arthritis. They came in wheelchairs from a nearby nursing home. One of the women could not even feed herself; she was bad off. He asked them if they came to get healed; they all nodded yes. First, Brother David laid hands on the head of the lady who couldn't feed herself. Within seconds of praying for her, her head stopped shaking! She looked up at Brother David and asked if he was Jesus. He laughed and said no, but Jesus was in him, and Jesus healed her. He told her she could get up; she did and started walking! Then she did a waltz-type dance for about an hour. While she danced, he looked at the other woman who said, "I'm ready." He prayed for her, and in a minute, she stood up. He then prayed for the man who took off running! "Tommy, I just stood there marveling at all three of them celebrating their healings."

Brother David also told me about a man in his mid-30s who had gum disease. It was so bad that his face was dark red and his teeth were black. So much poison in his body! After laying hands on him and praying three times, the redness disappeared from his face. When the man opened his mouth, his gums were turning pink and his teeth healed. When I was at Pisgah, I met that man's son, Bill. After several conversations with him, I finally had the nerve to ask if his dad had bad teeth when he died. He said that when he died, he had a full set of perfect teeth!

Brother David said that "when you came into Azusa, you got healed. The more you attended, the more faith you had, and the more things would happen. Because your faith was building up as you saw other people believing, soon you had no doubt when you walked up to someone that they were going to get healed."

Brother Brown

There were some saints who spent the remainder of their lives reliving the memories of Azusa Street. That's all well and good, but living is done in the present. In Philippians 3:13, Paul says that he forgets what is behind and strains toward what is ahead.

I met Brother Bill Brown in 1960. He had retired to Pisgah about six months before I got there. He lived with me in the dormitory. All he ever wanted to talk about was Azusa. Don't get me wrong! I loved the stories, but Brother Bill was always so sad because the Shekinah Glory had gone away, and the miracles at Azusa had stopped. But he told me some wonderful stories of miracles. He loved praying for those who were blind. While he was at Azusa, he participated in the healings of more than 50 blind people! He also told me stories of praying for miracles for the crippled and deformed; hundreds were healed.

I haven't told this one before. One night in 1908, a man came in who had suffered a stroke. He had to drag the whole left side of his body. He had no use of his left arm, and could hardly talk. He slurred and slobbered out of the left side of his mouth; he carried a big towel to wipe the slobber off. He told Brother Bill that he could see out of his left eye and breathe out of his left nostril, but that was all. Everything else was gone. Brother Bill said, "Let's pray and give God some glory. If God were to heal you and make you whole, God would get great glory." He laid hands on the man and started praying. The man twisted and jerked around. Within seconds, the man started dancing and shouting. He was instantly healed! Brother Bill said he danced and shouted with him.

At Pisgah, I actually got to meet that man. Brother Bill had written to him and asked him to come and meet this young man to whom the saints were telling their stories. He was very old, but healthy. I asked him what it was like before the Lord healed him. He said it was terrible; he had to have a big crutch. He would put it behind him and push on it, then drag his left leg up. He finally asked God to heal him or take him home. I asked the man what he ended up doing with his life. He said, "What do you think I did with my life?" I smiled and said that he probably became a reverend. He said yes, and he had retired from the ministry. God has it all planned out."

The day had started out rather somber, seeing Golgotha and thinking of the suffering our Lord had to endure. However, seeing the empty tomb brought it full circle. We ended the day rejoicing that our Savior is alive. There's no better feeling than to know you will spend eternity with Jesus!

At the place where Jesus was crucified, there was a garden and in the garden a new tomb, in which no one had ever been laid (John 19:41 NIV).

"Don't be alarmed," he said. "You are looking for Jesus the Nazarene, who was crucified. He has risen! He is not here. See the place where they laid him" (Mark 16:6 NIV).

For he has rescued us from the dominion of darkness and brought us into the kingdom of the Son he loves, in whom we have redemption, the forgiveness of sins (Colossians 1:13-14 NIV).

It became easy for me to detach myself from the course of life, so that while my hands and mind were engaged in the common affairs of every day, my spirit maintained its attitude of communion with God.

—John G. Lake

It is vain for us to pray while conscious that we have injured another. Let us first make amends to the injured one before we dare approach God at either the private or public altar.

—Jonathan Goforth

12

That's Us

*Going a little farther, he fell to the ground and prayed
that if possible the hour might pass from him. "Abba,
Father," he said, "everything is possible for you. Take this
cup from me. Yet not what I will, but what you will"*
(MARK 14:35-36 NIV).

The group of men quietly made their way through the rocky
landscape northeast of Jerusalem. The setting sun turned the sky
beautiful shades of pink and orange. Birds fluttered between the
old, gnarled olive trees. The area was populated with scrub and
limestone. The men were headed toward the Mount of Olives.
Their destination was a small garden at the foot of the mount,
the Garden of Gethsemane. The garden would provide a respite
for this weary crew who had been traveling up and down the

countryside of Israel. The leader of this band of brothers already knew what was ahead for Himself and the group in the coming week. Sadness and heartbreak pierced His soul.

❦

Making our way through the Kidron Valley to the Garden of Gethsemane and the Mount of Olives took more time than anticipated. In biblical times, this valley would have been filled with rocks and trees. Time and progress have taken their toll. Winding streets and noisy traffic was the order of the day. One has to make a concentrated effort to envision what it looked like 2,000 years ago. Though the exact location of Gethsemane cannot be determined with certainty, Greek, Latin, Armenian, and Russian churches have determined that this olive grove on the western slope of the Mount of Olives is the authentic site.

Some of the olive trees have been dated to 900 years old; others could be older. What is certain, is these amazing trees are offshoots from the same ones that were present in Jesus's day. They are still producing olives today. When we arrived at Gethsemane, the aura surrounding this holy place could be seen as well as felt. On the grounds of the Church of Nations, sitting at the foot of the Mount of Olives, the tranquil garden beckoned us to enter and contemplate for a while.

The garden is near the Church of Mary Magdalene. Close to the church is an old grotto where an ancient oil press still exists. Gethsemane means "oil press." Many scholars believe Jesus and His disciples spent the last week of His life here. Messiah means anointed one. Historically in Israel, kings were anointed with olive oil as a sign of being chosen and empowered by God to rule. In the Bible, Isaiah says that a *"shoot will come up from the stump of Jesse; from his roots a branch will bear fruit"* (Isaiah 11:1 NIV). It is only fitting that Jesus's last days were spent praying among the olive trees. After all, He is the anointed One.

Tommy said, "When I saw all those new shoots sticking out of the sides of those old, dark, olive trunks, I knew what they were. They were the wild olive branches. That's us, the Gentiles, grafted in! We are transplanted in there."

> *If some of the branches have been broken off, and you, though a wild olive shoot, have been grafted in among the others and now share in the nourishing sap from the olive root, do not consider yourself to be superior to those other branches. If you do, consider this: You do not support the root, but the root supports you* (Romans 11:17-18 NIV).

When Jesus prayed in the Garden of Gethsemane, He asked God to take the cup from Him. He knew He was going to die on the cross; but as a man, He was hoping that He would not have to suffer and experience so much pain. Our lives include some of these Gethsemane experiences. We know God's will, but our will wrestles with it. Yes, we want His will to be done, but sometimes it takes us awhile to get there. Jesus prayed several times in the garden until He came to the conclusion that God's will must be done.

We often have to pray a lot more than that, often never reaching that decision. Jesus knew the best place for Him to contemplate and pray was in the garden. We need to find our secret place to pray to give an advantage to our spirit, not our flesh. The place we commune with the Lord, can be a great influence on whether we obey God or ourselves. The more we make ourselves fully available to God, the more God makes His blessings fully available to us.

After a wonderful morning of prayer and once again releasing the call for revival throughout this country, we traveled up the Mount of Olives. On the way, Tommy told us some amazing stories of Brother Jonah.

AZUSA

Brother Jonah

"I really loved Brother Jonah. He wasn't one of the Azusa saints who lived at Pisgah, but he would come there and preach. He actually didn't preach his sermons; he would sing them! His daughter would play the piano, and he would start singing. He was in his 90s, but still very healthy. I loved it when I could catch him and convince him to sit down and tell me his stories.

Brother Jonah couldn't read or write. William Seymour told him to go sit down, pick up the Bible, open it and read it. He argued that he couldn't read. Seymour commanded him to open it and start saying what he saw. He did it. It took him about two months to read through the Old and New Testaments. He shut it and never opened it again, but he could quote anything in that Bible. He never missed! I would kid with him and would try to trip him up. He never got it wrong!

One night in 1909, Brother Jonah was down at the mission. A man came in who was very sickly looking. He wore a patch over one eye because he was blind in it. Brother Jonah asked to see the eye; it was dry and shriveled up. He asked the man to put the patch back on while they talked, and Brother Jonah prayed for the man's healing. After a bit, the man said his eye was feeling odd. They removed the patch; the eye was perfectly normal and he could see out of it!

One evening at Azusa, Brother Jonah sat there watching a little boy who had come in with his parents. He felt so sorry for the little fella because he was severely mentally ill. Brother Jonah started crying and said, "God, I know You love that little boy, and I think I am loving him, too." God told him to go over there and pray for the boy. The parents said they brought him to be healed and were so happy that Brother Jonah was going to pray for him. Brother Jonah told the parents that God had given him a message. The parents were supposed to keep bringing the boy to Azusa Street for prayer. They did, over and over for about four to five years! By that time, the boy was no longer mentally ill; he had become normal. I asked Brother Jonah what the boy was doing now (that was in the 1960s). He said he grew up and became a Harvard professor! Oh, dear Lord, yes!

Here's a story I have never told before! A really neat miracle that Brother Jonah was part of involved a middle-aged man who came in with his whole left side paralyzed. He could get up and walk a little bit, but usually just used a wheelchair. Brother Jonah asked him if he had suffered a stroke; the man said yes he had. "This came about because I didn't obey God," the man said. "God called me to the mission field, but I didn't want to go. I wanted to continue my life as a businessman. So, God got my attention. If He will heal me, then I will go to the mission field." Brother Jonah laid hands on him and prayed. He was healed instantly!

He went to Africa to the areas around Congo. He wanted to go into Congo, but got too old, so he came back to America. Eventually, his son told him that he would go into Congo to spread the gospel. I got to meet that man's son at Pisgah. He came and asked our preacher, Brother Smith, if Pisgah would sponsor him as a missionary. He was already 72 years old! He went to Congo and stayed three years. He established 350 churches there. When he started them, there were about 30-40 people in each congregation. Before he left, he took a tour of all the churches. They had grown to 300-400 people in each of them! That's in three years! That man was 75 years old when he came back. I tell people, don't tell me how old you are. You're never too old! If God says do something, go do it!"

⊱⊰

Being in the beautiful Garden of Gethsemane was a wonderful experience. The olive trees have been there for hundreds of years, being fed by the surrounding water to sustain them. Like those trees, we are also fed by the river of Zion. Through the heart of each believer is the river of God bringing new life and hope to us. Jesus spoke of rivers of living water flowing from the believer. It was time to visit the last place our Savior had been in Zion.

Our climb had brought us to the top of the majestic Mount of Olives.

Then Jesus went with his disciples to a place called Gethsemane, and he said to them, "Sit here while I go over there and pray" (Matthew 26:36 NIV).

And being in anguish, he prayed more earnestly, and his sweat was like drops of blood falling to the ground (Luke 22:44 NIV).

I will be like the dew to Israel; he will blossom like a lily. Like a cedar of Lebanon, he will send down his roots; his young shoots will grow. His splendor will be like an olive tree, his fragrance like a cedar of Lebanon (Hosea 14:5-6 NIV).

Nowhere can we get to know the holiness of God, and come under His influence and power, except in the inner chamber. It has been well said: "No man can expect to make progress in holiness who is not often and long alone with God."
—ANDREW MURRAY

For this time it will be God without disguise; something so overwhelming that it will strike either irresistible love or irresistible horror into every creature. It will be too late then to choose your side.
—C.S. LEWIS

13

Takes My Breath Away

Mount of Olives

Then the Lord will go out and fight against those
nations, as he fights on a day of battle. On that day
His feet will stand on the Mount of Olives, east of
Jerusalem, and the Mount of Olives will be split in two
from east to west, forming a great valley, with half of
the mountain moving north and half moving south
(Zechariah 14:3-4 NIV).

Their precious time together was coming to a close. Had it really
been 40 days ago since their Lord had risen from death? It
seemed like only yesterday they had watched the suffering and
horror of the crucifixion. One cannot explain the agony they had
gone through. However, their pain was short-lived, for Messiah
had risen! What glory! Jesus appeared to them, prophesying and

teaching. He spoke about the Kingdom of God. While enjoying a meal together, He gave them instructions to wait in Jerusalem; God had a gift to give them. They would be baptized with the Holy Spirit. The men whispered among themselves, wondering just what this meant.

The disciples followed their Lord up the Mount of Olives. Along the way, they reminisced about their numerous trips up this hill—past the tombs and the old trees, all the laughter and the tears. So much joy; so much pain. The time had come for Jesus to be seated beside His Father in Heaven. Thinking they could postpone His departure, the men asked as many questions as possible. They gathered around and asked Jesus if He was going to restore the kingdom to Israel at that time. With His usual patience, He told them that they would never know the times or dates of the end.

Jesus explained once more that they would receive power when the Holy Spirit came upon them saying, *"…you will be my witnesses in Jerusalem, and in all Judea and Samaria, and to the ends of the earth."* Upon this last statement, to their amazement, Messiah was taken up into the heavens, hidden by a cloud. The men fell to their knees in awe and reverence; they could barely breathe, let alone speak. They were filled with an indescribable joy, knowing their Lord and Savior would one day again set foot on this beautiful Mount of Olives. They waited. We wait. Come, Lord Jesus!

<>

The afternoon sun scorched the parched terrain as we ascended the mile-long ridge paralleling the eastern part of Jerusalem. The presence of the Holy Spirit was so strong as we sang hymns on the way up the Mount of Olives. We wondered how many praise songs had been sung on this hill through the centuries. Certainly, too many to count.

At 2,710 feet of elevation, the Mount of Olives overlooks Jerusalem and the Temple Mount. The mountain is first mentioned in Samuel when David is fleeing from Absalom. David wept as he went up the mountain because he had been betrayed by his son. In the days of the Second Temple, the religious ceremony marking the beginning of a new month was held on the mountain. After the destruction of the Second Temple, the festival of Sukkot was celebrated on the Mount of Olives. This Feast of Tabernacles celebrates the way God protected His people under harsh desert conditions when they wandered around, enroute to the Promised Land.

During the week of Sukkot, Jews made pilgrimages to the top of the mountain to overlook where the Temple once stood. This became a traditional place for lamenting the Temple's destruction. In the New Testament, the Mount of Olives is frequently mentioned as part of the route from Jerusalem to Bethany, located on the eastern side of the mountain.

A massive Jewish cemetery lies on the mountain. Burials began in it about 3,000 years ago and continue to this day. There are between 70,000-150,000 tombs. Jewish tradition holds that the Messiah will appear on the Mount of Olives and head toward the Temple Mount. The resurrection of the dead would start here, thus many in the Jewish faith want to be buried here, feet facing the Old City.

Tommy said, "I was astonished at the giant cemetery. It was a big shock to see all the tombs. I looked at Daniel, and said there were no flowers on them. He explained that they don't put flowers on these graves. They put rocks. When they crossed the

Jordan River, what did they put out there in the middle of that river? Twelve big rocks. The flowers fade away, but the rocks are still there. It dawned on me that the tombs go all around the mountain. They are there for when the Messiah comes; they believe that they will rise with Him. We know on the last day, the dead will rise."

We made our way to the parapet on top of the mountain. As Tommy looked out across the ancient city of Jerusalem and the Kidron Valley, God spoke mightily to him and gave him many visions.

Tommy

"I can hardly put into words what happened on the Mount of Olives. It blew me away! I didn't know how to handle it! I felt His presence around me and in me so strongly. I wanted to wait and see what He was saying to me exactly. I didn't want Tommy to get in the way. We get ahead of God. I thought, *This is it. This is where it's all going to take place!* I was sitting there and kept wondering if I should move farther up the mountain. I was ready to move up. God told me to move down. I moved several times until God said, This is the spot where I am going to put My foot!

God then let me see what was going to happen. I could see Him putting His foot down and that mountain splitting…the valley coming in. There was nothing under me; the mountain had split! I felt the earth come out from under me. Everything went through me; it took my breath a little. When I saw it, I reached up and grabbed the rail. It scared me; I wanted to shout right there! Until I realized I was having a vision, it frightened me. It was a great valley, very deep. It's about a mile. That mountain will move! I saw all these people walking.

I looked across toward Jerusalem and could see a little spot in the wall. It was the Eastern Gate. I couldn't take my eyes off that spot. God told me that after the mountain splits, Jesus will walk on level ground straight through that gate to receive His crown. We are all going to walk through that Eastern Gate. My mind was rushing 1,000 miles per hour! I could see it all coming before me. It was like a movie; I could see. It was mind-boggling. I was thinking that I had never seen any movie like that, so I wasn't reliving some movies I had ever seen. I guess God was just letting me see glimpses of the past…through history, the move of God, and how foolish man can be. How foolish.

I looked over and could see the history of Jerusalem. I saw Kings Saul and David, and so many others. Saul was a giant; the Bible says he stood head and shoulders above all of Israel. At one time, Saul was a prophet. There are some prophets who have messed up royally, even in our day. Watch and see what the prophets say. If it doesn't come to pass, you know the prophet just assumed. But if it does, you are supposed to fear that prophet. That doesn't mean be afraid of them, that means if they say something, respect it. I do that with prophets; I watch.

David wasn't very tall. David's friend Jonathan wasn't as tall as his father, Saul, but was quite a bit taller than David. I asked God where were David's brothers, then He showed them to me. I saw Samuel, God's anointed prophet, talking to David. Samuel looked like a prophet; I had to stand back and bow to him. I saw Solomon and his son. His son did not listen to the older men, so he lost ten tribes of the kingdom; that was sad. I saw Saul's daughter, Michal, and the three wives of David. Abigail was the prettiest; even prettier than Bathsheba.

I saw soldiers with swords, spears, bows, and arrows, but I didn't know who they were. Then I saw Nathan; I was most excited to see him and Samuel! The prophets had gray hair and beards; I was so drawn to them. They illuminated out to me. Samuel was the prophet who anointed King Saul and King David. Nathan was the prophet who anointed King Solomon. I continued sitting there, letting God talk to me. I felt like I was on a roller coaster. Even now, when I think of that vision, I find it hard to sleep. I go back to the Mount of Olives and see these people again. I keep seeing that vision over and over. It was incredible that God showed me where He will put His foot and how the mountain will split!

I was really amazed to sit there and see. I am not sure what all of it means, but I know we need to be ready. I think it will be soon! Why does God give some of us that ability? I always ask God a lot of questions. Maybe that's why God chose me for this. The only dumb question is the one you don't ask. Why He waited until I was 76 years old to show me, I don't know. God let me see what was going to happen! I thought, *This story has to be told!* He told me that I was supposed to get this into a book. I asked Him if Jody was the one to write the book, and I heard a resounding Yes! I know that those who bless Israel, will be blessed!"

Our time on the spectacular Mount of Olives was coming to a close. Walking among the beautiful olive trees allowed us to experience nature in the bustling city of Jerusalem. We had all been excited by the visions given to Tommy. Day after day, time after time, we will always be thrilled to hear from the Holy Spirit. It never gets old! We want to commune with our Lord as much as possible. It was becoming a tradition that as we traveled from place to place, Tommy would tell more amazing stories. That day we asked him to share stories about himself.

Tommy

"God loves everybody, and He will give everybody a chance. I'm glad I didn't pass mine by. I could have been out riding my horse, swimming, hunting, or fishing. Instead, I spent a lot of time in prayer meetings and revivals with my mother. When I was young, I didn't think my momma liked me. When I grew up, I asked my mom if I could take her out to eat, just the two of us; she said yes. At that meal, I told her that I was the oldest of 11 kids. She laughed, saying she was aware of that. I asked her why she dragged me to every healing evangelist she could get me to.

Some of my brothers and sisters didn't even know it happened. She told me she took me to the meetings so I could get the anointing of the evangelists. Wow! She knew God called me.

God will talk your language. My mother couldn't read or write; she was from the country. But God talked her language where she could understand. God doesn't have to talk to you the way you think He has to. He can speak any language He wants to speak. One day I told Marlene that if Jesus came and talked to her, He would speak the queen's English. But because I am a country boy from Oklahoma, He talks to me in the way I can understand it.

My mother had an incident with Kenneth Hagin in 1961. He was having a revival in Wright City, Texas, and every Thursday he had miracle night. Four of my brothers and sisters had gone over there and were baptized with the Holy Spirit, one at a time. Momma went over there saying she was going to get her healing from God. 'I'm going even if you have to carry me,' she said.

She had suffered from rheumatic fever and there were huge sores all over her. Brother Hagin prayed for her, telling his people to get paper towels to lay under her. People in the group said you could see a shiny spot on her forehead getting bigger and bigger, and could see her skin flopping. Right before their eyes, her face came off and a new one was in its place! Many years later, when she died, she still had the face of a 35-year-old woman. The rest of her was wrinkled, but her face wasn't. Those were the kind of miracles Brother Hagin had at his services, very similar to the ones at Azusa Street.

My grandma was a Baptist woman. You could have somebody bleeding from a wound; they would call for Grandma, and she would say, Okay, I'm going to quote my Scripture. But she would never quote it out loud. She would bow her head and say, 'God.' And every time, it worked! People would quit bleeding. One time, one of her grandsons got shot in the leg with a shotgun. They couldn't get the bleeding to stop. They called Grandma. She said, 'Okay, by the time you get back there to him, I will have prayed, and the bleeding will have stopped.' It had stopped!

Back in 1961, Johnny Bartleman, Frank's son, came to Pisgah. He was dying with a bad case of leukemia. He wanted prayer. Brother Smith, the pastor at Pisgah, told Johnny to get ahold of me. He said I was a hillbilly, but I had tremendous faith. I wasn't a hillbilly; I was just country.

Brother Smith told Johnny that I was with the Azusa Street saints a lot, and I was picking up their anointing. He came to me, and I prayed for him, but he didn't get healed. I asked him if there was somebody in his life that he just couldn't forgive. He said, yes, he couldn't forgive his father. I told him, 'God says that if you won't forgive, He won't forgive you. You're not going to get healed until you forgive your father. I know what you're talking about and your father was wrong; you've got to forgive him. Unforgiveness is poison. Why don't you go up to the mountain home and stay there awhile, until you can pray through?'

Now, here I am, an 18-year-old kid telling a 54-year-old man to go pray through! Johnny talked to Brother Smith, who sent him up to the mountain home. He stayed there for two months. When he came back, he said he had forgiven his father. I said let's see if he had. I prayed for him, and he was instantly healed! I smiled really big and said, 'Well, I do believe you forgave him.' I was so happy. I didn't understand a lot of that stuff, and I didn't realize what was going on. I didn't know I was going down in the history books! I just love stories, and I loved the saints' stories…and their lifestyles."

⊷⊶

God is our standard. He determines what is right and wrong, not culture. If you leave it up to humans, most will get it wrong every time. Our thoughts upon leaving the Mount of Olives is that one day, we will be back. There will be an open heaven above all of Jerusalem. On that day there will be a heavenly roar. The river of God's remnant will flow through the Eastern Gate, and we will be among them, following our glorious Savior!

Then the man brought me to the gate facing east, and I saw the glory of the God of Israel coming from the east. His voice was like the roar of rushing waters, and the land was radiant with his glory (Ezekiel 43:1-2 NIV).

He said to them: "It is not for you to know the times or dates the Father has set by his own authority. But you will receive power when the Holy Spirit comes on you; and you will be my witnesses in Jerusalem, and in all Judea and Samaria, and to the ends of the earth." After he said this, he was taken up before their very eyes, and a cloud hid him from their sight. They were looking intently up into the sky as he was going, when suddenly two men dressed in white stood beside them. "Men of Galilee," they said, "why do you stand here looking into the sky? This same Jesus, who has been taken from you into heaven, will come back in the same way you have seen him go into heaven" (Acts 1:7-11 NIV).

He said to them, "This is what I told you while I was still with you: Everything must be fulfilled that is written about me in the Law of Moses, the Prophets and the Psalms" (Luke 24:44 NIV).

Revival is something altogether different from evangelism on its highest level...revival is a moving of God in the community and suddenly the community becomes God conscious before a word is said by any man representing any special effort.

—DUNCAN CAMPBELL

The revival in South Wales is not of men, but of God. He has come very close to us...I am not the source of this revival but only one agent among what is growing to be a multitude. I wish no personal following, but only the world for Christ. The world will be swept by His Spirit as by a rushing, mighty wind. Many who are now silent Christians will lead the movement. They will see a great light, and will reflect this light to thousands more in darkness. Thousands will do more than we have accomplished, as God gives them power.

—EVAN ROBERTS

14

The Harvest

Do not treat prophecies with contempt
but test them all; hold on to what is good
(1 THESSALONIANS 5:20-21 NIV).

November 17, 2019

The night was a cold 27 degrees with thousands of stars sprinkled across the inky sky. I was sleeping soundly, nestled under an extra blanket. The clock ticked toward morning, although the sun was hours away from rising. The deep slumber would not last long. God needed to tell me something. With a start, I opened my eyes as the Holy Spirit told me three times softly, but distinctly:

"the sound of burning water"
"as clean as hyssop"
"restoring the giants"

At once, I began praying for the interpretation of these prophetic words. The Holy Spirit did not elaborate. I took out my Bible to search for a possible meaning…

THE PROPHETIC DREAM

The prophecy that Tommy Hicks gave over Tommy Welchel at Pisgah in 1962, stemmed from the following dream that Brother Hicks had. This incredible word from our heavenly Father speaks about the end-time harvest. As you recall, Brother Hicks told Tommy that he is one of the giants in this prophecy!

VISION OF THE BODY OF CHRIST AND THE END-TIME MINISTRIES

BROTHER TOMMY HICKS

"My message begins July 25, about 2:30 in the morning at Winnipeg, Canada. I had hardly fallen asleep when the vision and the revelation that God gave me came before me. The vision came three times, exactly in detail, the morning of July 25, 1961. I was so stirred and so moved by the revelation that this has changed my complete outlook upon the body of Christ, and upon the end-time ministries.

The greatest thing that the church of Jesus Christ has ever been given lies straight ahead! It is so hard to help men and women to realize and understand the thing that God is trying to give His people in the end-times.

I received a letter several weeks ago from one of our native evangelists down in Africa, down in Nairobi. This man and his wife were on their way to

Tanganyika. They could neither read nor could they write, but we had been supporting them for over two years. As they entered into the territory of Tanganyika, they came across a small village. The entire village was evacuating because of a plague that had hit the village. He came across natives who were weeping, and he asked them what was wrong.

They told him of their mother and father who had suddenly died, and they had been dead for three days. They had to leave. They were afraid to go in; they were leaving them in the cottage. He turned and asked them where they were. They pointed to the hut and he asked them to go with him, but they refused. They were afraid to go.

The man and his wife went to this little cottage and entered in where the man and woman had been dead for three days. He simply stretched forth his hand in the name of the Lord Jesus Christ, and spoke the man's name and the woman's name and said, "In the name of the Lord Jesus Christ, I command life to come back to your bodies." Instantaneously, these two heathen people who had never known Jesus Christ as their Savior sat up and immediately began to praise God. The Spirit and the power of God came into the life of those people.

To us that may seem strange and a phenomenon, but that is the beginning of these end-time ministries. God is going to take the do-nothings, the nobodies, the unheard-ofs, the no-accounts; He is going to take every man and every woman and He is going to give to them this outpouring of the Spirit of God!

In the book of Acts, we read that *In the last days,* God said, *I will pour out my Spirit upon all flesh* (see Acts 2:17 ESV). I wonder if we realized what He meant when God said, I will pour out my Spirit upon all flesh. I do not think I fully realized nor could I understand the fullness of it, and then I read from the book of Joel: *Be glad then, ye children of Zion, and rejoice in the Lord your God: for he hath given you the former rain moderately, and he will cause to come down for you the rain, the former rain, and then the latter rain…* (Joel 2:23 KJV). It is not only going to be the rain, the former rain and the latter rain, but He is going to give to His people in these last days a double portion of the power of God!

As the vision appeared to me after I was asleep, I suddenly found myself in a great high distance. Where I was, I do not know. But I was looking down upon the earth. Suddenly, the whole earth came into my view. Every nation, every kindred, every tongue came before my sight from the east and the west, the north and the south. I recognized every country and many cities that I had been in, and I was almost in fear and trembling as I beheld the great sight before me; and at that moment when the world came into view, it began to lightning and thunder.

As the lightning flashed over the face of the earth, my eyes went downward and I was facing the north. Suddenly, I beheld what looked like a great giant, and as I stared and looked at it, I was almost bewildered by the sight. It was so gigantic and so great! His feet seemed to reach to the north pole and his head to the south. Its arms were stretched from sea to sea. I could not even begin to understand whether this be a mountain or this be a giant; but as I watched, I suddenly beheld a great giant. I could see his head was struggling for life. He wanted to live, but his body was covered with debris from head to foot, and at times this great giant would move his body and act as though it would even raise up at times. And when it did, thousands of little creatures seemed to run away. Hideous creatures would run away from this giant, and when he would become calm, they would come back.

All of a sudden, this great giant lifted his hand toward Heaven, and then it lifted its other hand; and when it did, these creatures by the thousands seemed to flee away from this giant and go into the darkness of night.

Slowly this great giant began to rise; and as he did, his head and hands went into the clouds. As he rose to his feet, he seemed to have cleansed himself from the debris and filth that was upon him. He began to raise his hands into the heavens as though praising the Lord; and as he raised his hands, they went even unto the clouds.

Suddenly every cloud became silver, the most beautiful silver I have ever known. As I watched this phenomenon it was so great I could not even begin to understand what it all meant. I was so stirred as I watched it, and I cried unto the Lord and I said, "Oh Lord, what is the meaning of this?" And I felt as if I was actually in the Spirit and I could feel the presence of the Lord even as I was asleep.

And from those clouds suddenly there came great drops of liquid light raining down upon this mighty giant, and slowly, slowly, this giant began to melt, began to sink itself in the very earth itself. And as he melted, his whole form seemed to have melted upon the face of the earth, and this great rain began to come down. Liquid drops of light began to flood the very earth itself and as I watched this giant that seemed to melt, suddenly it became millions of people over the face of the earth. As I beheld the sight before me, people stood up all over the world! They were lifting their hands and they were praising the Lord.

At that very moment there came a great thunder that seemed to roar from the heavens. I turned my eyes toward the heavens and suddenly I saw a figure in white, in glistening white—the most glorious thing I have ever seen in my entire life! I did not see the face, but somehow, I knew it was the Lord Jesus Christ, and He stretched forth His hand, and as He did, He would stretch it forth to one, and to another, and to another. And as He stretched forth His hand upon the nations and the people of the world—men and women—as He pointed toward them, this liquid light seemed to flow from His hands into them, and mighty anointing of God came upon them, and those people began to go forth in the name of the Lord.

I do not know how long I watched it. It seemed it went into days and weeks and months. And I beheld this Christ as He continued to stretch forth His hand; but there was a tragedy. There were many people as He stretched forth His hand who refused the anointing of God and the call of God. I saw men and women I knew. People who I felt would certainly receive the call of God. But as He stretched forth His hand toward this one and toward that one, they simply bowed their head and began to back away. And each of those who seemed to bow down and back away, seemed to go into darkness. Blackness seemed to swallow them everywhere.

I was bewildered as I watched it, but these people whom He had anointed, hundreds of thousands of people all over the world, in Africa, England, Russia, China, America, all over the world, the anointing of God was upon these people as they went forward in the name of the Lord! I saw these men and women as they went forth. They were ditch diggers, they were washerwomen, they were rich men, they were poor men. I saw people who were bound with paralysis and sickness and blindness and deafness. As the Lord stretched forth to give them this anointing, they became well, they became healed, and they went forth!

And this is the miracle of it—this is the glorious miracle of it—those people would stretch forth their hands exactly as the Lord did, and it seemed as if there was the same liquid fire in their hands! As they stretched forth their hands they said, "According to my word, be thou made whole."

As these people continued in this mighty end-time ministry, I did not fully realize what it was, and I looked to the Lord and said, "What is the meaning of this?" And He said, "This is that which I will do in the last days. I will restore all that the canker-worm, the palmerworm, the caterpillar—I will re-store all that they have destroyed. This, My people, in the end-times will go forth. As a mighty army shall they sweep over the face of the earth!"

As I was at this great height, I could behold the whole world. I watched these people as they were going to and fro over the face of the earth. Sudden-ly, there was a man in Africa and in a moment, he was transported by the Spirit of God, and perhaps he was in Russia or China or America or some other place, and vice versa. All over the world these people went, and they came through fire, and through pes-tilence, and through famine. Neither fire nor perse-cution, nothing seemed to stop them.

Angry mobs came to them with swords and with guns. And like Jesus, they passed through the mul-titudes and they could not find them, but they went forth in the name of the Lord; and everywhere they stretched forth their hands, the sick were healed, the blind eyes were opened. There was not a long prayer, and after I had reviewed the vision many times in my mind, and I thought about it many times, I re-alized that I never saw a church, and I never saw or heard a denomination, yet these people were going in the name of the Lord of Hosts! Hallelujah!

As they marched forth in everything they did as the ministry of Christ in the end-times, these people were ministering to the multitudes over the face of the earth. Tens of thousands, even millions seemed to come to the Lord Jesus Christ as these people stood forth and gave the message of the Kingdom, of the coming Kingdom, in this last hour. It was so glorious, but it seems that there were those who rebelled, and they would become angry and they tried to attack the workers who were giving the message.

God is going to give the world a demonstration in this last hour as the world has never known! These men and women are of all walks of life, degrees will mean nothing. I saw these workers as they were going over the face of the earth. When one would stumble and fall, another would come and pick him up! There were no big I and little you, but every mountain was brought low and every valley was exalted, and they seemed to have one thing in common—there was a divine love, a divine love that seemed to flow forth from these people as they worked together and as they lived together. It was the most glorious night that I have ever known. Jesus Christ was the theme of their life. They continued and it seemed the days went by as I stood and beheld this sight. I could only cry, and sometimes I laughed. It was so wonderful as these people went throughout the face of the whole earth, bringing forth in this last end time.

As I watched from the very Heaven itself, there were times when great deluges of this liquid light seemed to fall upon great congregations, and that congregation would lift up their hands and seemingly praise God for hours and even days as the Spirit of God came upon them. God said, "I will pour My Spirit upon all flesh," and that is exactly this thing. And to every man and every woman who received this power, the anointing of God, the miracles of God, there was no ending to it.

We have talked about miracles. We have talked about signs and wonders, but I could not help but weep as I read again this morning, at 4 o'clock this morning, the letter from our native workers. This is only the evidence of the beginning for one man, a do-nothing, an unheard-of, who would go and stretch forth his hand and say, "In the name of the Lord Jesus Christ, I command life to flow into your body." I dropped to my knees and began to pray again, and I said, "Lord, I know that this time is coming soon!"

And then again, as these people were going about the face of the earth, a great persecution seemed to come from every angle.

Suddenly, there was another great clap of thunder, that seemed to resound around the world, and I heard again the Voice, the Voice that seemed to speak, "Now this is My people. This is My beloved bride!" And when the Voice spoke, I looked upon the earth and I could see the lakes and the mountains. The graves were opened and people from all over the world, the saints of all ages, seemed to be rising. And as they rose from the grave, suddenly all these people came from every direction. From the east and the west, from the north and south, and they seemed to be forming again this gigantic body. As the dead in

Christ seemed to be rising first, I could hardly comprehend it. It was so marvelous! It was so far beyond anything I could ever dream or think of.

But as this body suddenly began to form, and take shape again, it took shape again in the form of this mighty giant, but this time it was different. It was arrayed in the most beautiful gorgeous white. Its garments were without spot or wrinkle as its body began to form, and the people of all ages seemed to be gathered into this body, and slowly, slowly, as it began to form up into the very heavens above, the Lord Jesus came, and became the head, and I heard another clap of thunder that said, "This is My beloved bride for whom I have waited. She will come forth even tried by fire. This is she whom I have loved from the beginning of time!"

As I watched, my eyes suddenly turned to the far north, and I saw seemingly destruction: men and women in anguish and crying out, and buildings in destruction. Then I heard again, the fourth Voice that said, "Now is My wrath being poured out upon the face of the earth." From the ends of the whole world, the wrath of God seemed to be poured out, and it seemed that there were great vials of God's wrath being poured out upon the face of the earth. I can remember it as though it happened a moment ago. I shook and trembled as I beheld the awful sight of seeing the cities, and whole nations going down into destruction. I could hear the weeping and wailing. I could hear people crying. They seemed to cry as they went into caves, but the caves in the mountains opened up.

They leaped into water, but the water would not drown them. There was nothing that could destroy them. They were wanting to take their lives, but they could not. Then again, I turned my eyes to this glorious sight, this body arrayed in beautiful white, shining garments. Slowly, slowly, it began to lift from the earth, and as it did, I awoke. What a sight I had beheld! I had seen the end-time ministries—the last hour. Again on July 27, at 2:30 in the morning, the same revelation, the same vision came exactly as it did before.

My life has been changed as I realized that we are living in that end-time, for all over the world God is anointing men and women with this ministry. It will not be doctrine. It will not be a churchianity. It is going to be Jesus Christ. They will give forth the words of the Lord and are going to say, I heard it so many times in the vision, and according to my word it shall be done.

Oh, my people, listen to me. According to my word, it shall be done. We are going to be clothed with power and anointing from God. We won't have to preach sermons, we won't have to have persons heckle us in public. We won't have to depend on man, nor will we be denomination echoes—we will have the power of the living God. We will fear no one, but will go in the name of the Lord of Hosts!"

Tommy

"In 1961, Tommy Hicks, an Assemblies of God preacher, came to Pisgah. I had met him before. He asked me to walk with him along the Arroyo Seco River in Pasadena. From Pisgah, it was two hours up and two hours back. Brother Hicks had been called by God to preach in Argentina, back in 1954. On our walk, he told me about his trip including meeting Juan Peron, the dictator. Hicks wanted to ask him to use the radio station and a stadium for a revival meeting. After a lot of hassle, he finally got in to see him.

Compared to Brother Hicks, Peron was a huge man. Peron's face was eaten up with sores; Brother Hicks prayed for his skin. When Peron wiped his face with a towel then looked in the mirror, he was healed! He gladly gave permission to Brother Hicks to use one of the large stadiums for his crusade. He said, 'No, you can't rent the radio station; it is yours. You can't rent the stadium; it is yours. My limo will take you to the stadium and pick you up!'

During that revival, between 200,000 and 300,000 salvations took place. Thousands were healed. Brother Hicks is the one who started taking out his white handkerchief and waving it over the people; God would heal them. In Argentina, there is a life-sized statue of him.

Brother Hicks told me he would be back to Pisgah in a little while. Demos Shakarian took him around the world and wrote a book about it. That little while turned out to be a year; he came back to Pisgah in 1962. My lands, I'm 19 years old by now, but he took me on another walk down by the river, and he told me about the dream he had been having. Boy, I'm all ears! I'm liking this, you know. The end-time revival!

I was engrossed in the story, until he looked at me and said, One of those giants coming up out of the river will be you, Tommy. I got embarrassed; I could feel the back of my neck blushing.

I told him no, it was going to be somebody like him, Branham, Shakarian, Smith, DePlessis, Coe, or Allen. He said, 'Listen to me; don't take this lightly. It's not a coincidence that all of us so-called biggies want the Azusa saints to tell us their stories. They won't do it. What do you think that prophecy to you from Branham was about? When he said you're the one, be patient, and be obedient. Those saints banded together, and there's only one person they would tell their stories to. They are telling this country boy from Oklahoma. Tommy, all of us…we won't be there…you will be. Wait for God's timing; it won't be yours. It will be hard for you to be patient, but be patient.' I said okay.

Back then, Brother Sines said the secret is two things, patience and obedience. That's the same thing the Lord told me. That wasn't easy, especially for me. But over the years, I have become very patient. I have sat back; God has His time. Years later, Billye Brim told me that I was very young back then, and it would all happen quite a while later.

That used to boggle my mind—all these great men and women of God telling me things. I know God chooses, but I still think, *Why me?* I believe my God has everything lined out. That's why I don't worry. Stop and think. Tommy Hicks told me about me being one of those giants that came out of the river, in 1962. Almost

60 years ago. He said, We won't be here. None of them are here; they are all dead. But I'm here!

Satan tried to take me out. But I was already being used of God when he did that in 2010. That is a tremendous testimony. Technically, I was dead. I was a little confused. My heart wasn't beating…no pulse. I was sitting there talking to the doctors. They said they didn't know what was going on, but they were going to operate. I asked what chance did I have. They replied that I didn't have a chance, and I should be in the morgue right then. I started thinking about Heaven and wondering if I was going home. Not yet! I can see Tommy Hicks right now just as clearly as when he prophesied that to me. This is all starting to fill in! That prophecy is coming to pass; it just hasn't broken wide open yet. I don't know how much God is going to use me. Thing of it is, I believe this book will have a big influence in Israel and all over the world. But mainly revival is going to break loose in Israel, big time. We were in Israel in God's perfect timing. I waited until I got clearance from God. Wait for God's timing, and wait for the right person. Get the people hungry. A real hunger. It's starting to come up. Different ministries. The mountain has been melting down for some time. The rivers have been flowing. Now they are starting to come up out of the river. The miracles are happening in certain places of the world. But they will start exploding more and more! We've got to get the people to believe. Lots of people come to me and want to have the impartation. People from all around the world. One pastor came from Africa to meet me. He said he wanted my anointing so he could go back to Africa, and God will heal people of Ebola. Many were healed under that man. That's why people invite me places—to receive the impartation.

I was on the Gold Coast of Australia at a meeting. I prayed for a man who was limping. They had to carry him down the steps. He had been hurt in a motorcycle accident, and they had to put rods in to knit his legs together. Steel rods going through his knees. I prayed for him, then went on praying for other people. I got through, sat down, and looked up. I saw the man going up and down the steps—running. He was running up and down, shouting. He ran back to me and pulled his pant legs up to show me his legs. I said, 'What about it?' He told me that before, he couldn't walk up or down the stairs. He had to be carried. He was now able to run because the rods were gone! I would call that a miracle like they had at Azusa Street.

I was invited to Arlington, Virginia. A man had purchased a private school. It wasn't a Christian school, but the man worked in religion. Before, he had come to see me, and his wife had gotten healed. He knew he had gotten an anointing, an impartation. The man said he would pay my way to Virginia if I would come to the school. He asked me what it would take for revival to break loose in this school. I said, 'One undisputed miracle. Everybody would know that if that certain person got healed, it would have to be God.' The man said he had someone.

There was a young man there, 18 years old, who was in his senior year of school. He was extremely bow-legged. Walked terribly. I asked him how old he was when it started, and he said he was about 4 years old. I said, 'Now, you're going to see a miracle!' We put two seats facing each other. I sat in one; he sat in the other. I told him to put his hands in my hands, and said, 'Now let's see God work a miracle.' I was just doing what God told me. His feet started jerking. It took about 15 minutes. Little by little his feet were coming in. They came together, and I asked him if he could move his feet. He said yes. I asked him if he had ever run. He said, 'No. You saw how hard it was for me to walk.' He had a girlfriend; she was crying. Lots of the boys and girls were yelling, 'Look at that!' I asked if they had a place where he could run.

There was a 200-foot long hallway, so I asked the people to clear out of the way and turned him loose. He made three laps down and back. Needless to say, they had a revival! Those people had no training or teaching at all on healing. God did that. I told the young man, 'Now, listen to me, tomorrow those feet will try and start coming back together, but you have the authority over it to command it to stop. By His stripes, you were healed. And if you were, you are! Satan will try to steal it from you.' People there were wondering why God took so long to heal the boy. I told them He wanted all of them to see it happen.

I was recently in Chile at a meeting. I kept saying that God was going to use the little kids. The pastor of the kids' church wondered why no one ministers to the young ones. The preacher was bringing the children up onto the platform where I was. They were almost running over each other, trying to get up there. They wanted to touch my face. There was a girl around 10 years old who was paralyzed. Through the translator, I told the father to put her on my lap. He did, and she just lay there watching me. I smiled and whispered in her ear, 'The Bible says you are healed!' Then they took her back to her seat.

Not too much longer, we took a break. I was going to the restroom. There was a steep hill that most people couldn't walk up. I'd say at least half the people there couldn't walk up it. They had stairs, but I couldn't climb that many stairs, so they drove me down there and back every time. When I came out of the restroom, I looked across the drive and there stood that little girl with her parents. I just froze. Here she came walking across the road to me! She motioned for me to bend down, so I did, and she kissed me on the cheek. She said something; I looked at the translator and asked what the girl had said. She said, 'I am going to walk up the hill. She walked up that hill! They put me in the truck to watch what was happening, but I was crying so hard that I couldn't see. When she got to the top, she started jumping up and down, screaming something. I asked what she was hollering. The translator said, Brother Tommy, she is saying, 'The Bible says I am healed!'

That broke that revival wide open! I said, Listen guys, I didn't heal her. I just obeyed the Bible and prayed for her. The anointing did the work. The only doctrine I teach is *'these signs shall follow.'* The other two teachers quit preaching and went to praying for the sick. I would only speak about ten minutes and then would have a prayer line. The other guys started doing the same thing. We should never stop praying for the sick. What is the meaning of miracles? It's for the unbelievers. So many thousands came to God during the healing revivals. Thousands came to the altar when they saw these miracles. We had miracles galore!

Brother Dave and some of the other people there were crying. Later, I asked them what they had been crying about. They said that when I was up there telling the Azusa stories, my face was glowing. That's why the kids wanted to get up there to touch my face. The little girl was the one supernatural, unquestionable, undeniable miracle. The Shekinah Glory is falling on Chile!

I could fill books with all the wonderful miracles I've seen. I have traveled the world and have seen hundreds of miracles. Jody has seen so many through her prayers, too! That's one reason the Lord brought us together. I know the impartation from the Azusa Street saints is for Jody. God is using her mightily, and she is also part of the Tommy Hicks prophecy. I am passing my mantle to her. There will be an outpouring of God's Spirit throughout Israel and all over the world. It will be like nothing we've ever experienced. The bride of Christ is waking up—the giants are rising up out of the river!"

❦

Looking back on that cold November morning of 2019, Tommy and I now understand what the Holy Spirit was speaking to me. He woke me with these prophetic words, to prepare me for what He had called me to do. It was part of the Tommy Hicks prophecy. *"The sound of burning water"* is the liquid fire falling. The liquid drops of light passed from the Lord to His people. This anointing will be used to heal the sick, the desperate, and the lost. *"As clean as hyssop"* is the Church, the bride of Christ, being cleansed and prepared for His return. In the Bible, hyssop was used to sprinkle blood on the doorframes of the Israelites for protection, so the destroyer would not strike the firstborn of that family. Hyssop was also used to dip into wine vinegar to give Jesus a drink while He was on the cross, according to John. God is calling us to a deeper walk of repentance and surrender. *"Restoring the giants"* is the remnant rising from the river. We are the ones He is restoring and calling to go throughout the world. We are the remnant of Christ, who He will use supernaturally for miracles, signs, and wonders!

We—you, Tommy, me—are the Church. We are the giants spreading the Gospel around the globe! In these end-times, we are called to drink of the living water of God, then go throughout the world sharing His Good News. There is a purpose and a destiny we all have to fulfill!

The Lord had woven my part in the tapestry years before I was born. What an honor to walk beside Tommy, truly one of the giants. It is so humbling to know that God has a plan for me in this end-time revival. He has a plan for you, too! Jump into His river! To God be the glory!

Cleanse me with hyssop, and I will be clean; wash me, and I will be whiter than snow (Psalm 51:7 NIV).

For prophecy never had its origin in the human will, but prophets, though human, spoke from God as they were carried along by the Holy Spirit (2 Peter 1:21 NIV).

So Christ himself gave the apostles, the prophets, the evangelists, the pastors and teachers, to equip his people for works of service, so that the body of Christ may be built up until we all reach unity in the faith and in the knowledge of the Son of God and become mature, attaining to the whole measure of the fullness of Christ (Ephesians 4:11-13 NIV).

There are only two days on my calendar. This day and that day.

—MARTIN LUTHER

Let God's people everywhere see His plan, and begin to seek in deep, true humility. Then He will reveal Himself and His plan to them. One man with the real power of God upon him can do more than a thousand who go on their own account. Only those who are true and loyal to God and His present day message will share in this great victory. The company who really humble themselves and stand the test, God will use to do His work.

—WILLIAM H. DURHAM

Conclusion

We Believe

Then Jesus came to them and said, "All authority in heaven and on earth has been given to me. Therefore go and make disciples of all nations, baptizing them in the name of the Father and of the Son and of the Holy Spirit, and teaching them to obey everything I have commanded you. And surely I am with you always, to the very end of the age" (MATTHEW 28:18-20 NIV).

The fire that fell at Pentecost did not remain in that upper room. This river of God's fire began as a stream, expanded, and then became a great torrent. The Holy Spirit swept through the nations, changing the hearts and minds of billions. He is the living fire ready to take hold of all believers right now.

I believe there is a reason this book is in your hands. You did not arrive at this moment by accident. These stories are not just history. They are not about reliving the past, but honoring it. We are not here just to tell other people's stories, but to be living and writing our own stories. The fire that originated in Jerusalem and flared again at Azusa has been building. Now is the time to walk in our authority and power. It's time to dwell in the realm of all possibilities!

Like the saints of Azusa, hold your position, knowing that Heaven will respond. Be humble and repent; have faith. Prayer is one of the keys to revival—for those giants to rise from the river. God's people need to be on their knees. Cry out to God to help you follow His plan for your life. Embrace that plan. Run strong with it, and do mighty deeds in Jesus's name. Let that still, small voice be the loudest voice in your life!

Tommy said, "My God has everything laid out. That's why I don't worry. I pray then turn it over to God; it's not my problem anymore. There is always a way. I have never found faith to fail, never once. May the Holy Ghost give us a new touch of faith in God's power. May we have a living faith that will dare to trust Him and say we believe. The biggest miracle is salvation. There's plenty of room in Heaven."

Revival changes everything. It can be costly and inconvenient—our selfish desires become irrelevant. There is no room for pride and ego. Revival brings death to your old life; new life springs forth. God wants a fountain to flow in your life. A stream of holiness, power, and mercy—out of you will flow rivers of living water! We prayed in every city we visited in Israel, raising our hands throughout the country for revival for this great nation. Since we are praying for revival, we need to be ready for what God is releasing. Revival is no longer a question—it is happening. Today, Israel and other nations are experiencing an incredible move of God. The remnant has awakened; the giants are rising! Get ready for more miracles, signs, and wonders!

Tommy said, "The end-time revival prophecies are starting. The prophecies from Seymour, Wigglesworth, Parham, Hicks, and others are coming to pass. You will see them spring up all around the world. I love these testimonies of the Azusa Street saints. You see, the book of Acts is the only book in the Bible that doesn't have an 'amen.' That's because it has never ended. It's the acts of the apostles; we're still in that book. I think we should be recording and printing the acts. I don't believe God's through."

And so, the rivers merge—Zion, Azusa, Oklahoma, Kentucky. Since the beginning of time, God's hand has directed our paths. His great love for us is beyond all understanding. There is no love like His, no compassion like His. To be loved is the cry of every human heart. He hears your cry. Are you ready? Jesus is waiting for you. May the Lord give us a new vision of Himself, a fresh touch of divine life and His presence.

It has been an honor and a privilege to share our journey with you. May you be blessed by the stories of the dear saints and the miraculous moves of God. May the visions that the Holy Spirit gave Tommy in Israel bring joy and a hunger for revival into your life. And, may a longing stir within you to visit God's Holy Land!

Our time in the Holy Land is over. But it's not the end. The best is yet to come! As we say, "Next year in Jerusalem!"

"Look, I am coming soon! My reward is with me, and I will give to each person according to what they have done. I am the Alpha and the Omega, the First and the Last, the Beginning and the End" (Revelation 22:12-13 NIV).

—YESHUA HAMASHIACH

About the Authors

Tommy Welchel is a leading historian on revival. He has been known as the last living link to the Azusa Street Revival. As a young man, he lived with the saints who attended that incredible outpouring. For six years, they shared the stories of God's miracles with him. He tells those stories around the globe, and miracles follow. He resides in Arizona with his wife, Marlene.

⋈✦⋈

Jody Keck is a revivalist and founder of Upper Room Ministry. She is an international speaker who flows in the miraculous. She has a strong prophetic anointing and has been known as a woman walking in God's supernatural power. Her passion is sharing the Gospel of Jesus, and her revelation of His glory inspires people around the world. She resides in Kentucky with her husband, Steve.

JODY KECK MINISTRIES

P.O. Box 1348

Somerset, Kentucky 42502

jodykeckministries.org

*If you would like more information
about Tommy and Jody, please visit our
website, or contact us at the address above.*

YOUR Prophetic COMMUNITY

Are you passionate about hearing God's voice, walking with Jesus, and experiencing the power of the Holy Spirit?

Destiny Image is a community of believers with a passion for equipping and encouraging you to live the prophetic, supernatural life you were created for!

We offer a fresh helping of practical articles, dynamic podcasts, and powerful videos from respected, Spirit-empowered, Christian leaders to fuel the holy fire within you.

Sign up now to get awesome content delivered to your inbox
destinyimage.com/sign-up

 Destiny Image